The Protestant Presence in Twentieth-Century America

SUNY Series in Religion, Culture, and Society
Wade Clark Roof, editor

The Protestant Presence in Twentieth-Century America

Religion and Political Culture

Phillip E. Hammond

STATE UNIVERSITY OF NEW YORK PRESS

Published by
State University of New York Press, Albany

© 1992 State University of New York

For information, address the State University of New York Press,
State University Plaza, Albany, NY 12246

Library of Congress Cataloging-in-Publication Data

Hammond, Phillip E.
    The Protestant presence in twentieth-century America : religion
and political culture / Phillip E. Hammond.
        p.   cm. — (SUNY series in religion, culture, and society)
    Includes bibliographical references and index.
    ISBN 0-7914-1121-4 (alk. paper). — ISBN 0-7914-1122-2 (pbk. :
alk. paper)
    1. Protestant churches—United States—History—20th century.
2. United States—Church history—20th century. 3. Christianity and
politics—History—20th century. 4. Christianity and culture-
-History—20th century. I. Title. II. Series.
BR515.H334   1992
280'.4'09730904—dc20   91-31731
                                                                                        CIP

10 9 8 7 6 5 4 3 2 1

Contents

Introduction   1

Preface: Religious Pluralism and Social Order   9

PART ONE: THEMES FROM THE PAST

1.   In Search of a Protestant Twentieth Century: 27
American Religion and Power Since 1900

2.   The Moral Majority and All That: 43
The Curious Path of Conservative Protestantism

3.   Cults and the Civil Religion: A Tale of Two Centuries   55
(co-authored by Robert Gordon-McCutchan)

PART TWO: EVANGELICALISM AND POLITICS

4. An Approach to the Political Meaning of   69
    Evangelicalism in Present-Day America

5. Political Evangelicalism: 81
    The Anglo-American Comparison

PART THREE: RELIGION AND LAW

6. The Courts and Secular Humanism: 95
    How to Misinterpret Church-State Issues

7. The Shifting Meaning of a Wall of Separation: 108
    Some Notes on Church, State, and Conscience

8. Constitutional Faith, Legitimating Myth,   118
    and Civil Religion

PART FOUR: THE TRAJECTORY OF RELIGION AND
POLITICAL CULTURE

9. Religion and the Persistence of Identity   137

10. Up and Down with the National Faith   152

11. The Fate of Liberal Protestantism in America   163

Notes   173

References   185

Index   193

Introduction

What remains to be said about the relationship of Protestantism and political culture in America? The best answer is "Everything and nothing." *Nothing* more can be said because a saturation point has been reached using the time-honored, but worn-out, concepts of the past. Until new concepts arrive to provide significantly different perspectives, we are not likely to do more than rearrange yesterday's analyses. Thus, the very promising discussion inspired by Robert Bellah's reintroduction of Rousseau's civil religion notion—a discussion, incidentally, in which I was an enthusiastic participant—has faded into obscurity. Bellah's recent book, *Habits of the Heart*, does not even invoke the term, largely, I think, because others adopted it but then perverted it by trying to force it into traditional molds. The civil religion idea was, among other things, an effort to encourage new thinking about religion and politics in America, but much of the resulting conversation dissolved into arguments over whether civil religion exists and, if so, whether it differs from unenlightened patriotism. I concluded that the repeated efforts to clear away misunderstandings were not worth whatever advantage the term yields and thus I, too, have largely stopped using the term, though on occasion the following essays will employ it. On the other hand, *everything* remains to be said about Protestantism and political culture in America because many of the presuppositions— inspired by secularization models of society—have proved singularly inadequate to account for the resurgence of (especially) certain kinds of Protestantism in contemporary American life.

The essays of this book represent what I hope are realistic responses to this anomalous situation. They are intended to continue an ongoing dialogue as if some of the apparatus for joining religion and culture still works, but they also acknowledge the unexpected features of the current scene. Who, after all, anticipated that mainline Protestantism would experience a generational decline after 1965? Or who, in postwar America thought that, twenty years later, Liberal Protestants would cry "foul play" at Conservative Protestant incursions into the political arena? Something has obviously been rearranged in the American religiopolitical scene. Liberal Protestantism remains in some sense the "established" religion in America, for example, but somehow its caretaker role has disappeared. Catholics and Jews may still call for equal time in the public arena, but Protestants can no longer be regarded—by themselves or others—as occupying preferred status in national life. No longer is it for them to "grant" equal time to Catholics and Jews, for example. Protestantism thus stands in an altered relationship with American culture, but what is that relationship? Where, to put it in the terms of this book's title, do we find Protestantism present in twentieth-century America?

AN AUTOBIOGRAPHICAL NOTE

One might regard my own intellectual odyssey as an effort to answer this question. Coming from a long line of Methodist clergy, I attended— with great pleasure and benefit, though with little thought to any alternative education—a Methodist college, a college much caught up in the dilemma of how to retain religious distinction while still laying claim to producing intellectual elites in a pluralistic society. That dilemma hit me particularly hard, as I felt genuinely motivated by the religious forces of family, tradition, and culture, even as I came to admire academic life. I "preenrolled" in seminary.

In an experience that can be described only in conversion terms, however, I realized the folly of my clerical aspiration. I understood little of the basis of my realization at the time, of course—my recollection is that I foresaw that my sermons would be preached to deaf ears—but in retrospect I think I was beginning to comprehend the ambiguous role Protestantism was playing in twentieth-century America. In any event, I gave up the plan to go to seminary and graduated with a major in speech and drama, plus a vague hope that some day I would be a college professor.

After a few years as a secondary-school teacher of speech and English, during which time I sampled summer and night school courses in the various behavioral sciences, I decided on sociology as the discipline allowing me the greatest flexibility in studying the subjects that interested me. I recall drawing up a list of "master" issues I wanted to pursue, all of which were no doubt naively framed. In retrospect I can see that they revolved around the question of how people—and especially *societies* of people—arrive at their conceptions of good and evil. From a slightly different perspective, this question can be seen as the same one that dissuaded me from the ministry.

As luck—not foreknowledge—would have it, I went for graduate study to Columbia University, where I encountered Charles Y. Glock and the sociology of religion, relatedly trying to understand the "religious revival" of the 1950s. Those were exciting times, as Glock was applying to the study of religion some of the newly refined tools of social research, chiefly those developed in social surveys. I wrote a dissertation, in fact, using some newly collected survey data from the Congregational Church (now the United Church of Christ) to explore the issue of whether people's religious beliefs made any difference in their church-going, or whether such beliefs were essentially irrelevant. Entitled *The Role of Ideology in Church Participation* (published, two decades later, by Arno Press as part of a Dissertation Series), I found that theological views were something of a factor, but not much.

The first postdoctoral research I undertook led to the publication of *The Campus Clergyman*. While it is exaggerated to say that this investigation was on the path of my "master" question, nonetheless one can readily detect in that research my interest in how or whether Protestantism was maintaining a presence in culture. Here again, incidentally, analysis revealed not a portrait as church theory would have it but a picture of struggle just to remain alive in the domain of higher education that, only a few decades before, Protestantism had dominated.

From graduate school days onward, then, I had begun to frame the master question in several ways. In addition to asking how and

why Liberal Protestantism has lost moral suasion, I was also wondering
where, if at all among social institutions, might moral suasion be found.
One answer, given tentative expression in a 1963 essay, was the court
system, and in several ways I began to explore the possible meanings of
this answer in the event it were, so to speak, correct.

My next monograph *(The School Prayer Decisions: From Court Policy
to Local Practice)*, written with the political scientist Kenneth Dolbeare,
was thus an effort to gauge the Supreme Court's capacity to influence
American culture's notions of good and bad. Public school religious
practices of various kinds, which had once been quite standard, were
now opposed by some, regarded as necessary by others. Knowing, from
our own surveys as well as others', that great regional variation existed
before the Supreme Court rulings of 1962 and 1963 and knowing that in
some places compliance with the Court's rulings appeared widespread
and in others defiance existed, we set out to understand why and how
the difference. In a manner reminiscent of Protestantism's dubious influence, we found that regardless of official pronouncements, compliance
or noncompliance on this matter seemed little influenced by the Court's
moral suasion.

About this time Bellah published his seminal essay on America's
civil religion, and I realized that my own musings and research found
focus under that rubric. Several endeavors, including an extended stay
in Mexico, were devoted to investigating the conditions that allowed or
encouraged religion and politics to fuse in some sense. The written
expressions of these endeavors were published along with an equal
number of Robert Bellah's essays, in our coauthored *Varieties of Civil
Religion*. By now, of course, I had deviated considerably from the master
question of where and how societies arrive at decisions of good and
bad, but it is fair to characterize even the deviation as bearing on the
wider issue of moral currents in our culture: where they come from,
where they are going, and what they sweep along in their flow.

THE BATTLE WON AND THE BATTLE LOST

Liberal Protestantism surely remains among those currents, but so does
Evangelical Protestantism, increasingly so, it seems. And so does the
legal system. How are we to understand this situation? One thing seems
certain: Protestantism's present ambiguous relationship with American culture is itself a product of Protestantism's earlier dominance of

that culture. That is to say, the weakness now seeming to characterize mainline Protestantism, as well as the robustness seeming to characterize Evangelical Protestantism, both result from the very success Protestantism had in convincing Americans that the church is a voluntary association, that all should be free to worship God in their own way, and that therefore neither doctrinal orthodoxy nor church membership should be a factor in cultural decisions of right and wrong. I would add that therefore the legal system increased in importance as religious pluralism prevailed.

Even if one comes to this radical pluralism through a profound conviction that God intends people to live pluralistically, one cannot persuade (let alone force) others to believe in pluralism *because* God ordains it. And yet Protestantism, when it was dominant, somehow managed—largely through the ethic of fair play as transmitted by public schools, no doubt—to infuse American culture with this fundamentally Protestant idea. As a result, Protestantism lost its peculiar relationship with that culture. Its present "failure" is thus a product of its previous "success."

Unlike a zero-sum situation, however, unusual complications arose in this case. Although it might be said of public education in the nineteenth century that Protestantism's gain was in some sense Roman Catholicism's loss, it is also correct to say that Protestantism's success in institutionalizing the pluralism ethic made winners of all religions, especially large minority religions, and made losers of all religions, especially Liberal Protestantism that might, under other circumstances, have retained the privileged position it now no longer has. Thus the winner, in winning, also lost.

These essays are responses to one or another of three questions that can be asked of this battle won but also lost. One question asks how Protestantism's altered relationship with American culture came about and how Protestantism therefore became Liberal Protestantism. The second question asks how, in this transformation, Evangelical Protestantism came into being and how, in the face of modernity, it remains so resilient. The first encourages looks backward, whereas the second encourages looks toward the future. The first focuses on Liberal Protestantism itself, the second obviously strays into other territory, and the third question thus involves this "other territory": the arena of courts and jurisprudence.

The individual essays cannot easily be allocated to one category only, however, because all three questions must be posed simultaneously. One cannot understand Liberal Protestantism's present relationship with American culture without understanding its past, an obvious enough statement. But neither can one understand Evangelical Protestantism's current situation without understanding Liberal Protestantism's past and especially its altered relationship with American culture. Likewise, one understands neither Liberal nor Evangelical Protestantism without recognizing their changing relationships with the legal-political sphere. Therefore, even if some of the following essays are more "historical" and others more "contemporary," they all have behind them this backdrop of Protestantism and the political culture. There is even, I would like to think, some continuity in the essays as a group; I want here merely to identify what I believe to be this thread of continuity.

We begin with a Prelude, a general view of the impact of religious pluralism on religion's relationship to society and culture. Pluralism, it argues, changes the very nature of this relationship. This is a general argument, providing a theoretical context for the rest of the essays.

Chapter One looks at the overall development of Liberal Protestantism from mid-nineteenth century onward. It identifies the watershed period around the turn of the century that led to the creation of Liberal and non-Liberal Protestantism, but its primary concern is with what happened to the Liberal wing.

Chapter Two, by contrast, follows the path taken by the non-Liberal wing (and discusses the ensuing problem of nomenclature, incidentally). In a sense, then, one might say of these two chapters that they contain at least most of the "seed ideas" to be found in later chapters.

Chapter Three, ostensibly on cults and thus an apparent change of direction, is in fact an exercise in analysis of Protestantism's relationship with culture when the relationship is treated as a variable—now closer, now more distant. What might, in the first third of the nineteenth century, be seen as a relationship so close as to make for a vibrant American "civil religion," by the 1970s, is seen as a poorly articulated, if not badly mauled, civil religion.

Chapter Four reviews the analysis Tocqueville made of the political consequences of America's (evangelical) religion in 1831. It then applies to the current evangelical resurgence in America this same analysis. Will the consequences of today's revival resemble the consequences of the earlier revival? The answer suggested is No.

Chapter Five starts with the observation that, until the 1970s, developments in England and the United States among Evangelical Protestants had been parallel and mutually supportive. Since then, however, Americans of this religious persuasion have been politicized, while their English counterparts have not. This difference is explored and explained.

Chapters Six, Seven, and Eight discuss religious culture as it is dealt with in the court system of the United States. Chapter Six is an argument with those who find "secular humanism" to be a discrete, coherent ideology rather than—as I contend—an inevitable vocabulary arising from pluralistic circumstances; whereas Seven, also concerned with court-related vocabulary, argues that the metaphor of a wall of separation between church and state is a metaphor with a changing meaning as the legal implications of religious pluralism change over time in America. Chapter Eight, originally an extended review essay, tries to show that profound religious issues underlie matters quite removed from the arena of churches as commonly understood.

Chapters Nine, Ten, and Eleven return to the book's main theme: the relationship of religion and political culture. Chapter Nine is an effort—programmatic indeed—to state the ways in which religion, whether liberal or conservative, intersects the sense of personal identity. If, indeed, religion generally, and Protestantism specifically, have undergone a shift in relationship to American culture and politics, then clearly this shift should be evident in the ways people think of themselves. The most recent of all of these essays, Chapter Nine outlines the research I subsequently carried out and saw published as *Religion and Personal Autonomy*. I have therefore added a coda to this chapter, indicating how that research modified my original thinking. Chapter Ten goes back over the historical picture to project two hypothetical futures, depending on the ultimate significance of American religious developments since 1965. I predict the gloomy one. The final chapter can be interpreted just as gloomily, perhaps, though that is not its purpose. Rather it is intended as a realistic appraisal of Liberal Protestantism's past and present relationship with American culture. As such, it serves as something of a "summary" or "conclusion" to the essays preceding it. In summarizing and concluding, it is not therefore pessimistic, for the appraisal reveals grounds for hope and modes of action as well.

The "master" question dating back to my youthful years—how societies arrive at notions of good and evil—although thus not answered in these essays, nevertheless is hovering around somewhere. I have long since given up the illusion that it ever will be finally answered, of course, but the conviction lingers that the question should always be explored and tentative resolutions offered. As announced at the outset, therefore, both everything and nothing yet remains to be said about the relationship of Protestantism and culture. I do not conclude that the scholarly endeavor is therefore pointless. Among other things, as I now want to make clear, the endeavor itself has put me in effervescent company.

One of my colleagues invokes the term *sparkling* when searching for a superlative to describe a fellow academic: whether it is that person's teaching, research and writing, or academic citizenship. *Sparkling* is a wonderful adjective because it captures the spirit of what those of us privileged to live our lives in the academy most prize in each other: the effervescent capacity simultaneously to be enticed, enthused, even enthralled by one's colleagues' ideas while, at the same time, feeling that on occasion we might entice, enthuse, and enthrall in return. My colleagues in Religious Studies at UCSB perform this legerdemain routinely, to a point where even the most cynical admit that something sparkling regularly occurs. In 1978 I was invited to join this unusual band, and have never regretted my decision to say yes. To those colleagues, therefore—retired, continuing, and since joined—I offer these essays.

I have also enjoyed the support of the Lilly Endowment and its officer, Robert Wood Lynn, now retired, who enabled many of these essays to come into being. My gratitude is great.

Preface: Religious Pluralism and Social Order

I know a married couple who, every morning of the year, eat corn flakes for breakfast, but he insists on Kellogg's Corn Flakes, and she will eat only Post Toasties. They live harmoniously, of course; what sane person would start a war over breakfast cereal? The very absurdity of a corn flake conflict highlights a profound question nonetheless: Why is it that pluralism of some things, such as breakfast cereal, carries no implications for the social order, whereas pluralism of other things, such as religion, has profound implications for the way people live together?

The obvious answer has to do with the "importance" of various things in our lives, ranging from the utterly trivial to matters of life and death, including life after death. With trivial matters we can be readily pluralistic, yet multiple views on important issues give pause. A people's knowledge that their views of salvation are incompatible, for example, very likely engenders hostility among them.

Buy why? Why is an acknowledged difference in taste in salvation doctrines important, whereas a difference in taste in breakfast cereals is not? After all, a breakfaster could *claim* that cereal is the lodestar of his life, and who could deny it?

I

"Importance" in this context, it would seem, exists along two related, though conceptually separate, dimensions. One of these we can call *sovereignty*, the other *centrality*. By sovereignty is meant essentially authority, although it is authority in the broadest sense, including its very informal exercise. Parents have sovereignty over children, bosses over workers, police over citizens, teachers over pupils, and so forth. Not all sovereignty is recognized in law, and genuine disagreement may exist in a group concerning the legitimacy with which sovereignty is exercised. But at base it is a structural feature of a situation, resting not on the acceptance of any particular person but on the acceptance of people generally. Without this general acceptance, importance along the sovereignty dimension does not exist.

Thus parents are important because society makes them important, and this is true irrespective of the private sentiments of particular parents and children. For this reason, therefore, having a plurality of parents, as in the case of children of remarried divorced parents or of "in-law" obligations, is often times stressful and, potentially at least, productive of conflict and breakdown in social order. Even a mother and father can, by making contradictory authoritative pronouncements to their child, create disorder in a household.

The dimension called here *centrality* expresses importance in quite another way, even though empirically it frequently accompanies sovereignty. Unlike sovereignty, which is structural, centrality is personal; people significantly determine for themselves how central in their lives is an issue, event, thing, or person. They have a say in how much their lives will be organized around these matters. Conceivably, our breakfast eater could make cereal centrally important in his life, but he could not assign it sovereignty.

One person's notions of importance, however, are likely to correspond with other persons' notions of importance, which explains the degree of overlap between centrality and sovereignty. But where individual variation from the group along the sovereignty dimension is regarded as deviant, such individual variation is allowed—perhaps even encouraged—along the centrality dimension. Thus, sports activity may remain central in the life of an athlete long after graduation, and long after such activity possessed sovereignty as well, as it probably did when the athlete was a student. A multiplicity of sporting activities in the lives of adults is not likely to disrupt the social order, therefore, inasmuch as adults are largely free to make those activities only as central as they elect. Pluralism of sports in the lives of high school students, on the other hand, can raise havoc with the status order, scheduling of hours, and competition for talent. Students cannot ignore the sovereignty of sports, so to speak; it has a kind of importance for their ordered lives that the centrality of sports later on will lack.

These observations are hardly new. All introductory textbooks in sociology cover this material, though they may do so in bewilderingly different ways. Power, authority, legitimacy, status sets, ideology, symbol system, the stranger, urbanization, secularism, visibility—an enormous range of concepts might be employed in the discussion of these ideas. They bear, after all, on the question giving rise to the discipline of sociology itself: How is social order possible when so much evidence suggests we might more likely be at each other's throats? What, to return to the opening image, keeps pluralistic breakfast eaters from going to war over corn flakes? To answer that corn flakes lack importance, that they have neither sovereignty nor centrality, provides us with some of the terms helpful in a discussion of religious pluralism.

Max Weber supplies us with still other helpful terms in his comparative studies of religion. All religions deal with "salvation," he noted, and thus are necessarily important. But they differ in their views of the role played by life on earth in reaching salvation, and differ thus in their importance *for social order.* Some religions, for instance, regard a believer's years on earth as basically unrelated to his or her ultimate destiny (Weber called these religions *other-worldly mystical*), whereas other religions make future salvation contingent precisely on the record established in this life (Weber called these *inner-worldly ascetic* religions).[1] The importance of religion for social order is consequently much greater in the case of inner-worldly ascetic religions; along especially the sovereignty dimension, they are more important in the *social* lives of their adherents than are other-worldly mystical religions in the *social* lives of their adherents.

From the standpoint of pluralism and social order, then, we would expect *less* disruption of the social order when religions of an other-worldly mystical sort appear together in a single society. Correlatively, if one or more inner-worldly ascetic religions coexist with one or more other religions, we might expect *more* social disorder. Certainly "holy wars" are more characteristic of the West, whose religions—Judaism, Christianity, and Islam—have been relatively more inner-worldly and ascetic. Religions of the East—Hinduism, Buddhism, Confucianism,

Taoism—being relatively more other-worldly and mystical, have erupted less often in sacred battles.

A substantial consequence of this greater tendency in the West for friction to accompany religious pluralism was the development of a religiopolitical arrangement called in the United States the "separation of church and state." The motives of the framers and ratifiers of the American Bill of Rights were no doubt mixed—some more concerned to keep government out of religion, others more fearful of church entanglement in politics—but all were faced with the unavoidable presence in their new nation of multiple expressions of faith. A similar situation, already present in England, was met with a somewhat different solution; so, too, in Holland and later France. By now, however, all "Western" nations have, in effect, separated church from state.

But an irony thus follows. It has already been said that Judaism and (especially Protestant) Christianity, being inner-worldly ascetic, tend to have more important implications for the social lives of their followers. (A leader once said he would sooner face a legion with swords drawn than a lone Calvinist armed with an open Bible.) When such religions exist pluralistically, however, and therefore are subject to "separation" from the state, the effect is precisely to mute the social (not necessarily the individual) consequences of each religion, rendering it less important for social order.

The path of religion in modern Western history has thus been one of aggressive social assertion in the name of religion, accompanied by political maneuvers to minimize the sovereign (and thus possibly, though not necessarily, the central) importance of religion. The history of the separation of church and state in the United States has taken just this path, as we shall now review.

II

America was religiously plural from the outset. As Sidney E. Mead said: "the remarkable thing about the English settlements in America is that there, in the brief period between 1607 and 1787 these traditionally antagonistic groups of people learned to dwell side by side in relative peace."[2] It is also true that those "antagonistic groups" were overwhelmingly Protestant and Calvinist, so we might imagine there was less pluralism in actuality than in name. Nonetheless, antagonism existed, and—important to the argument here—whatever harmony was achieved by these various religious groups was a harmony *secured not by finding a common religious outlook but by recourse to government*. Thus, even in the early years of the Massachusetts colony, with an "established" Puritan church, many Anglican, Baptist, and Quaker colonists sought and found relief by appealing to secular political authorities.

Here was an early instance of the irony referred to earlier. The effort to ensure religious liberty—that is, to allow religions to exercise the importance they claim in people's lives—enlarged the role of secular government in erstwhile religious affairs, thereby muting the social consequences of those religions. They lose in sovereignty and (potentially) in centrality. Michael Novak expressed the irony this way: "No one church was allowed to become the official guardian of the central symbols of the United States. Instead, the nation itself began to fill the vacuum where in many cultures a church would be."[3]

This ironic process went another step in late eighteenth- and early nineteenth-century America. Despite their diversity, churches and clergy had exercised considerable authority in community matters through much of the 1700s. With the First Great Awakening (c. 1730-1760) and especially the Second (c. 1800-1830), however, churches relinquished a good deal of that authority. Orthodoxy of any sort was made vulnerable by these two waves of religious fervor, which, by emphasizing emotion in religion, thereby deemphasized doctrine, instruction, prescribed ritual, even denomination. Certainly, too, clerical authority in the wider community was compromised in these revivals, however strategic individual clergy may have been in the religious experiences of their flocks.

It is not that religion was without effect; the revivals' impact on such social institutions as education, health care, journalism, reform movements, and so on, are well known. It is rather that religion became undeniably *voluntary* and in becoming voluntary further lost sovereignty, even as it may have gained centrality in some lives. The freer people were to be religious in their own way, the less important it became *how* they were religious or even *if*. The government, in protecting and expanding religious liberty, was acknowledging the crucial nature of religion among a multireligious people; simultaneously and necessarily, it was rendering religion less crucial for the social order.

There is no doubt that nineteenth-century America experienced a vast multiplication of religions. Not only did Protestant groups proliferate, Jews increased in number, and Roman Catholics came in massive waves. Meanwhile Transcendentalists, Spiritualists, Millerites, Mormons, and many more added to the obvious religious heterogeneity. All would, in due time at least, establish their right to exist and propagate. Pluralism took a quantum leap during this period.

Nothing, however, symbolizes the irony of religious pluralism as does a Supreme Court case at the end of this period. In 1879 (in *Reynolds v. United States*) the Court decided on the matter of Mormon polygamy. May Mormons "profess belief" in polygamy? Yes, of course, the Court implied. But "Can a man excuse his practices . . . because of his religious belief?" asked Chief Justice Waite in his written opinion. No, came the answer. "To permit this would be to make the professed doctrines of religious belief superior to the law of the land." Polygamy was outlawed.

Now, Protestant theory of the state had earlier joined with Enlightenment democratic theory because of the near identity in the two theories concerning the rights people hold *prior* to the rights granted to them by any government. Enlightenment democratic theory conceived such rights as "natural" and self-evident, and Protestantism understood by them persons' duties to God, with which no government may interfere. As government increased the range of religious beliefs falling under its protection, however, it necessarily encountered duties to God, like polygamy, that it would not recognize as valid. One can see in the next century the range of "duties" allowed and disallowed, from conscientious objection to sabbath observance to blood transfusion refusal to ritual snake handling. It must be appreciated, however, that the very freedom to invoke religious sanction for (unconventional?) behavior on the grounds of religion's centrality in persons' lives—and the frequency with which such claims *are* allowed—is the same "freedom" that diminishes the sovereignty of religion. In fact it is the government that grants the license; believers (or church, etc.) may *claim* a prior right but may not automatically exercise it in the name of religion. And, of course, the rest of us need not share their belief in their *prior* right.

This problem was recognized early on in America. By mid-eighteenth century a "Puritan principle" was understood to mean: "The civil Power hath no jurisdiction over the Sentiments or Opinions of the subject, till such Opinions break out into Actions prejudicial to the Community, and then it is not the Opinion but the Action that is the Object of our Punishment."[4] It is just that with every increase in the variety of religious "Opinions" allowed, this dilemma came more sharply into focus.

An occasion for sharpening the focus yet another time came during the next century, which further diminished the social importance of religion. Pluralization this time meant not so much an increase in creeds, however, as it meant giving noncreeds competitive footing. Henry May states the situation this way: "In the late nineteenth century a series of painful shocks jolted the American people toward a realization of profound change. Suddenly or gradually, many were forced to realize that they were no longer living in an agrarian democracy, but in an industrial nation already increasingly dominated by giant corporations."[5] The case could be made even stronger; before the Civil War, America had a "Protestant" culture, its images and symbols drawn largely from Protestant sources, however varied. Non-Protestant substitutes, if acknowledged at all, were "permitted" by a cultural elite still dominated by Protestants.

By the turn of the century, however, the cultural elite was no longer Protestant-dominated, and neither were the challenges to Protestantism simply other religions. They included noncreedal programs (e.g., socialism), as well as compelling alternatives to historic creeds (e.g., evolutionary implications for biblical interpretation). Moreover, these challenges penetrated every major denomination in Protestantism (and performed analogous subversions in Judaism and Catholicism). A direct effect of these challenges was the emergence of "liberal" religion, well symbolized by the creation in 1908 of the Federal Council of Churches. An indirect effect was the acknowledgment by these churches that, when it came to influencing society, they would now have to slug it out with other persons and groups having "equal" footing.

A new level of pluralistic awareness had been reached, then. Although the upshot in Protestantism (the so-called Social Gospel movement) was clearly a move in the inner-worldly ascetic direction—as the church tried new ways to make its presence felt in redeeming the world—so, too, did it mean a further reduction in religion's hegemony. By moving further into the world to influence it, religion once again had to bargain away still more if its sovereignty. Now, for example, churches would share eleemosynary efforts with secular governments, abiding by the rules set by the latter.

This shift is illustrated by Protestantism's experience with the labor union question: from adamant rejection of unionism at the outset, coupled with limited appeal to the emerging working classes, to hearty embrace several decades later, coupled with a recognition that government, not the church, administers the labor law. The working classes, incidentally, did not queue up for Protestantism as a result of this transition, so one might argue that centrality as well as sovereignty was lost.

The next "period"[6] takes us to the near present. From early in the twentieth century until the 1950s, at least two parallel pluralizing forces developed: one more organizational, the other more theological. The organizational force was exemplified by the National Conference of Christians and Jews (which began corporate life as the National Conference of Jews and Christians). An early (1932) report complained that:

> In some places the school system is essentially still a Protestant school system: celebration of the Christian holidays is taken as a matter of course; "good character" in the appointment of teachers is interpreted as involving membership in a Protestant Church; . . . [W]hile there may be little open hostility toward Jews or Catholics, the teaching is imbued with an exclusive nativism that creates suspicion for everything that does not fit into the local tradition.[7]

That same report asserted wistfully that believers need not relinquish what is distinctive in their creeds to cooperate in removing religious hostility.

But what if "celebration of Christian holidays" or "Protestant teachers" are exactly what Protestants claim *is* distinctive about their creed? What if such claims are made as prior duties to God? The report ignored this possibility. That is to say, questions of *how* to pursue the spirit of brotherhood in the context of religious pluralism were simply avoided. When, after Hitlerism and the Holocaust, the hard questions could not be ignored, they were answered (by mainline denominations anyway) in such a fashion as to (1) extend full religious rights to Jews, but (2) therefore demote what was historically distinctive about Christianity.

This kind of abrupt recognition that a leap in level of pluralization had occurred is seen in the about-face experience of Supreme Court Justice William O. Douglas. In 1952 (in *Zorach* v. *Clauson*, a case allowing for released-time off-campus religious instruction in public schools) he wrote for the majority that "We are a religious people whose institutions presuppose a Supreme Being." But just thirteen years later (concurring with the majority in *U.S.* v. *Seeger*, which allowed the claims of an agnostic conscientious objector), Douglas wrote: "Does a Buddhist believe in 'God' or a 'Supreme Being'? . . . When the present [conscientious objection] Act was adopted in 1948 we were a nation of Buddhists, Confucianists, and Taoists, as well as Christians. Hawaii was indeed filled with Buddhists. . . ."

A parallel theological force showed up at the same time, though less abruptly. From the beginning of the century, religious liberals were charged with forsaking what was distinctive about their tradition. "Let us be honest with ourselves," wrote one reviewer in a typical expression of this criticism, "Let us face the question whether Christianity is a supernatural religion or not, whether it is from heaven or of men, whether it is the absolute religion or simply the purest form of religion that has yet appeared in the development of history."[8] To defend Christianity as but the "best yet" not only opened the possibility of a better alternative still to come; it also meant that any debate would be carried on in language transcending Christian language. Religion would be justified by science, for example, raising the question whether science was not then the true religion, with Christianity and other faiths being reduced to its alternative expressions. Here was a genuine dilemma for religious liberals.

In 1954, for example, Reinhold Nieburhr addressed this dilemma in a panel convened to discuss Religion and Freedom of Thought: "if we define religion as the self's commitment to some system of meaning, or its loyalty to some scheme of values, we must accept the fact that there is a basic contradiction between religion and the freedom of the mind."[9] That is to say, one cannot be ultimately committed to multiple creeds; if Jew and Christian (or Buddhist and Hindu, etc.) therefore coexist harmoniously in a single society, they *must* be committed to "some system of meaning" more ultimate than Judaism or Christianity. Evangelicals in our own day (who seem intent on restoring nineteenth-century Protestant America) are essentially correct on this one point at least: What they call "secular humanism" *has* replaced Christian vocabulary as the major language of most of society's movers and shakers. In what other language *could* a rationale for a religiously diverse people be expressed?

Needless to say, this leap in understanding of the social consequences of pluralism did not mean that Protestantism could no longer serve as compass to the Protestant, Catholicism as anchor for the Catholic, and so forth. But it did mean the *social* importance of these faiths was diminished. More sovereignty had been lost.

We come, then, to the present period, marked by the realization, first, that there really is but one world, though it contains many kinds of beliefs and, second, that a number of these "other" beliefs are now firmly entrenched in America. Many persons still have a difficult time *expressing* their expanded notion of religious toleration. Relinquishing one set of commitments for another is difficult to do in public, difficult maybe even to recognize in private. Thus, the World Council of Churches in 1961 agreed: "Christians see religious liberty as a consequence of God's creative work, of his redemption of man in Christ, and his calling of men into his service. Accordingly human attempts by legal enactment or by pressure of social custom to coerce or to eliminate faith are violations of the fundamental ways of God with men."[10] Only a few years later, Catholics would express it more candidly in a statement emanating from Vatican II:

> the human person has a right to religious freedom . . . all men
> are to be immune from coercion on the part of individuals or of
> social groups or of any human power. . . . [I]n matters religious
> no one is to be forced to act in a manner contrary to his own
> beliefs, whether privately or publicly, whether alone or in asso
> ciation with others, within due limits.

But whether a statement begins (as does the World Council's) with a particularistic "justification" before announcing the universal creed or instead states the universal creed outright (as the Catholics did), the message is clear: In the face of expanding religious pluralism, we uphold religious liberty as a value taking precedence over any of our particularistic creeds.

Not all modern world citizens are committed to this universal creed of religious liberty. Certainly there are some in the United States who would constrain Popery by law, who regard Jews as beyond salvation, and who view devotion to a Swami, chanting on street corners, or living in a commune as just further evidence the world is in its last days. But institutions, especially legal institutions, function in reasonable accord with the creed of religious liberty. Except for occasional reverses—which are, of course, wrenching experiences for those involved, and may mobilize efforts by others to reinvigorate the creed— the modern Western world lives religiously in relative harmony.[11] It is correct to assume, therefore, that religion is even less important—in sovereignty, if not centrality—in those societies in which it is found in such plural forms.

III

Loss in sovereignty occurs in two ways. One of these, the "privitizing" of religion, is often noted about religion in modern society. *Privatization* of religion as a concept is meaningful, of course, only under the circumstance of religious pluralism, but, at the same time, religious pluralism imposes such privatization. Because we may believe anything we like, we are therefore entitled to keep it to ourselves. Thus, most churches no longer take seriously the affirmation of creeds, Sunday School literature is as likely to teach about other faiths as it is to instill its own faith, and probes into another's beliefs are considered impolite. Just as, by law, religious belief is irrelevant to school admission, employment, and marriage licensing, so has it become irrelevant for the Methodist Church, say, to inquire *how* Methodist a member's beliefs might be. In fact, forces even discourage the Methodist Church from being very explicit about what Methodist doctrine *is*.

But what is one's right to keep private thus becomes unavailable as justification in making a social claim. Along with privatization, then, comes the moral *neutralization* of religion. People's rights are not diminished, but the rights they can claim in the name of their religion are. This situation has the effect, in law, of substituting "conscience" for religion, and courts assess the sincerity and social cost—not the substance or correctness—of belief, which is to say that one belief is, substantively, as good as another as far as the law is concerned.

Privatization plus neutralization equals reduced sovereignty, so it can be said that, with these two conditions, religion plays less of a structural role in society's deliberations. What is off limits for me to inquire about is off limits for you to invoke, and the religious liberty that developed alongside religious pluralization had both these effects: it did away with religious tests, heresy trials, and religious discrimination, but it also rendered religion less important along the dimension of sovereignty.

Because sovereignty and centrality are empirically related, however, we must inquire whether increased religious liberty also means decreased centrality of religion. I will argue here that it does, and that only in this fashion do we understand properly the so-called religious renewal of the current day.

In asserting the reduced centrality of religion I do not mean to judge the authenticity of anybody's religious commitment. How central in a person's life is his faith is a question ultimately answerable in this world only by that person. Nonetheless, *declaration* of centrality need not be the same thing as actual centrality, and in this ideological corner, too, persons may be serious in their declaration without recognizing its unreality. At any rate, with the undeniable loss in religion's sovereignty, we might expect an accompanying diminution in centrality. How might that occur?

Loss of centrality, like loss of sovereignty, takes two forms. One of these may be labeled *ritualization*, the other by the awkward but apt term *commodification*. *Ritualization* refers here not to liturgical matters but to the increasingly clear differentiation between times when one is "being" religious and when one is not. The analogue is found in drama, wherein audiences suspend the reality of their lives outside the theater to adopt the reality inside the theater. The effect can be powerful, of course, but the absence of links to the rest of life is nevertheless obvious, and suspicion is aroused by any implication to the contrary. Visitors to Disneyland know ritualization intimately; once the gates are entered, it is a fantasy world one willingly participates in. And departure is just as clear a ritual.

Now, of course, for those who operate the rides, don the makeup, or preach the sermons, there is no "suspended" reality. Instead they have schedules to make, demands to meet, and so on. And so it *can* be with those who come through the church door. *But it need not be*; and that is the point. Churches, like Disneyland, have certainly accommodated members so as to interfere as little as possible in the rest of their lives, a charge seemingly embarrassing to churches but that indicates they recognize the same modern forces Disneyland does, with its parking facilities, nursery, wheelchairs, and shovel brigade behind the horse-drawn streetcars. One can participate meaningfully without disrupting one's life otherwise. As in attending a baseball game, one can cheer, experience victory or despair, and enjoy the equivalent of a hot dog. But when the service ends, it is back to "real" life. Religion is ritualized.

Commodification need not seem so cynical. It refers to the loss in centrality that accompanies the proliferation of any product. Religious pluralization represents proliferation, needless to say, thus accenting for every "consumer" the fact that one's choice of brand *is one's choice*. The Baptist thus comes to realize that Baptism may be *his* preference, but so, too, does the Catholic have *her* preference, the Witness *his*, and so forth. The effect is to make switching brands easy, as every longitudinal study of denominational affiliation makes clear.

The term *commodification* is appropriate here because religion is being commercialized, not just in the sense that it has economic interests it must protect (which has always been true), but also in the sense that each religion competes knowingly in a marketplace with other religions. People thus "consume" religion, making it a commodity competing for their time, energy, money, and loyalty. Just as consumers can be fiercely committed to Brand X soap although recognizing that other consumers are just as fiercely committed to Brand Y, so can people "choose" a religion in a commodities marketplace, all the while knowing their brand loyalty *is* of their own making. How else is one to understand a finding that 75 percent of Lutherans agree salvation is only through belief in Jesus Christ, whereas 75 percent also agree all of the world's religions probably recognize one and the same God?[12]

Of course, with loss in religious sovereignty (through privitization and neutralization), the loss in religious centrality (through ritualization and commodification) carries less consequence for society. Loss in sovereignty insulates religion, so to speak, which renders religion's centrality—at whatever level it may be—less crucial for social life. If, as some may want to argue, evangelical religion has increased in centrality in the current day, it is still the case that, because of lower sovereignty, such increase is as inconsequential as would be a decrease. Despite the rhetoric, in other words, a group like the Moral Majority could *sound* the way it did because nobody had to listen. There is evidence that few did, despite the mass media's fascination. By the time the press discovered Falwell, for example, his following had already started to decline.[13]

IV

Where, then, does this leave the relationship between religion and social order? Several observations might be made in conclusion.

First, the adjustments to religious pluralism in America meant a decreasingly sovereign role for religion, perhaps especially those adjustments made in the twentieth century. The benefit was continued religious participation in social affairs, but by mid-century—following the New Deal legislation and, somewhat later, the Great Society legislation—it was clear that any Protestant, Catholic, or Jewish social agenda was now not only shared with nonreligious interest groups but also administered chiefly by political parties. That is to say, religion's impact on society was diffused through political institutions, thereby losing its distinctively religious identity. Although one cannot call Social Security, the FDIC, Unemployment Benefits, or Civil Rights Acts "religious," one can nonetheless recognize them as brotherhood universalized by pluralism: enacted by public (not church) officials, upheld by common (not canon) law, and administered by secular (not sacred) government. To the degree such legislation has preserved social order through the tumult of the last fifty years, one can say religious pluralism therefore contributed to social order.

Second, religious pluralism is the ecclesiastical equivalent of capitalism. Religious liberty for each person is like the freedom to contract for anything in the marketplace; and it is not surprising that churches have on occasion succumbed to the marketplace mentality, offering religion for profit. A more serious point, however, is that churches in this century are among those who have viewed with alarm the marketplace logic taken to extreme—what Robert Bellah calls "utilitarian individualism."[14] Having earlier believed laissez-faire doctrine to be nature's law, churches in the mainstream elected to stay "in" the world by repudiating their earlier defense of unbridled capitalism. By taking this inner-worldly ascetic step, religion lost sovereignty, as we saw earlier, but it stayed in the arena and remained in position to exercise some influence on social order, therefore.[15]

That leaves, third, the obvious possibility that societies do not require "common values," contrary to much of social scientific theory. Social order may not rest on common acceptance of a set of substantive values but rather on at least minimal acceptance of a set of procedures.[16] We have seen that, as it pluralizes, religion necessarily diminishes in social importance. And yet religions (as corporate bodies) have not been without relevance for social order. Rather, they have taken their places alongside other influences, prepared to compete on equal terms. By thus accepting the set of procedures adopted by others, religion retains some clout, even as it is, of course, demeaned. But it could hardly be otherwise in the context of multiple religions.

Finally, all that has been said regarding pluralistic America has assumed inner-worldly ascetic religions, religions that want and need to influence society. An alternative is for religions to move in the direction of other-worldly mysticism, to turn inward, shunning worldly concerns. It seems unlikely that all of American culture will make such a radical shift, the momentum of hundreds, if not thousands, of years being too strong. Yet surely it is not coincidence that Asian-flavored religions have recently become popular, with certain sectors of America anyway. In 1976, for example, it was calculated that followers of Maharishi Mahesh Yogi in America exceeded the number of Jews.[17] In percentage terms that is not large, but neither can it be dismissed as unimportant. Moreover, evangelicalism, which has remained numerically strong despite its low visibility until recent decades, has elements of other-worldly mysticism, not meditative certainly but world rejecting nonetheless.

Of course, no matter how sizeable world rejection might become it would still exert little influence on society because of its unconcern for society's issues. The historical situation is likely to remain, therefore; so-called mainline religions will continue to influence social order but in diminished capacity, a diminished capacity arising from the conditions of religious pluralism.

V

The foregoing pages were written in the early 1980s, an essay to lay out a conceptual scheme for understanding how the relationship between religion and political culture may change. All of the following essays, written at that time or since, might be seen as explorations on this theme. Each in some way examines the shifting sovereignty or centrality of Protestant religion and therefore Protestantism's capacity to influence political thought and action in the United States.

The essays of Part One thus trace the fading sovereignty of liberal Protestantism and the fluctuating centrality of conservative Protestantism. Part Two looks directly at the political ramifications of resurgent conservative Protestantism and compares the situation in Great Britain and the United States in this regard.

In one sense, the essays of Part Three depart from the analysis of Protestantism but only if Protestantism's meaning is restricted to churches. The meaning of Protestantism, it is argued in the three essays of Part Three, is also found in American legal institutions, which have gained in sovereignty and centrality as the ecclesiastical expressions of Protestantism have done otherwise. Part Four then returns to these ecclesiastical expressions and conjectures in several ways about what the future may hold.

It must be acknowledged that the essays making up the eleven chapters of this book were not in the mind of the author when this Preface was being written. Indeed, the occasions prompting these diverse articles were themselves so diverse that it might be said that each was drafted independently. Of course, that is not literally the case, so the reader will find some repetition of themes and illustrations that would not occur had the first chapter been written with the last chapter in mind. Nonetheless, anyone interested in connections between religion and politics will, I hope, find food for thought in the pages that follow.

Part One

Themes from the Past

1

In Search of a Protestant Twentieth Century: American Religion and Power Since 1900

As was the case with many students of American religion, my interest in conservative Protestantism was brought about by rapidly overwhelming events. I had assumed that the point of view variously called evangelical, fundamentalist, holiness, Pentecostal, or millenarian was moribund in America. I found it hard to see Billy Graham as more than vestigial, to see itinerant revival and healing shows as more than chicanery, and to see so-called Christian schools as other than crabby devices used by new members of the middle-class to shelter their children from the facts of ethnic life. After all, the Rev. Dr. Graham found Richard Nixon's profanity his most offensive feature, and Christian schools seemed to draw disproportionately from the muscular, Bible-quotin' people who, especially if they drove to church in pick-up trucks, seemed to be suffering delusions of gender. The whole conservative religious scene, in other words, was out of step with the America I knew. Therefore it could be dismissed. And dismiss it I did.

As Stephen Warner (1979) warned us, however, people like myself held these opinions at considerable intellectual cost. We were unable, given this outlook, to understand many of the real motives possessed by followers of evangelicalism; we were blinded to the real sociopolitical impact such groups might have; and we could not even guess that, by 1980, all three major candidates for President of the United States would declare themselves "born again," as religious revivals melded into political campaigns. That is to say, conservative Protestantism is—and perhaps for some decades has been—a force of cultural importance, and I was among those not seeing it. I decided to educate myself by backing up to the nineteenth century, to search out the roots of this contemporary phenomenon.

My first aim here, then, is to summarize what I learned from going back 100 years. I shall argue that the changes undertaken 70 to 110 years ago by Protestantism were monumental, that among these changes was the breaking of the link between Protestantism and power in America, a link that had been quite strong for most of the nineteenth century. I want second, therefore, to show how this breakup was manifested in both domestic and foreign church affairs. Third and finally, I turn to the conservative resurgence in our day, claiming it is best understood not as dissatisfaction with turn-of-the-century *theological* changes but as dissatisfaction with the *cultural* consequences brought on, in part, by those theological changes. My title, "In Search of a Protestant Twentieth Century," thus has two distinct meanings: It refers to the futility of efforts by liberal Protestantism any longer to play a distinctively sovereign role in American political life. And it refers to equally futile efforts by conservative Protestantism, profoundly unhappy with this broken relationship between religion and power, to find programs yet in this century on which it can hang the label *Christian*.

THE MONUMENTAL CHANGES IN PROTESTANTISM

As students of social structure, we sociologists know that social change comes in lurches. Persons and cultures may undergo steady change, but institutionalized patterns of interaction tend to remain fairly constant until some event causes people to redefine their relationships. A new standard procedure then appears as these relationships get restructured.

I rehearse this obvious point before discussing the monumental changes made by American Protestantism during the late nineteenth and early twentieth centuries because I am well aware that any ideas claimed to be new can, in fact, be found earlier in somebody, somewhere. Some intellectual historians delight in just such neverending backpedaling, and maybe without them we would err in believing all ideas are constantly being reinvented. Nevertheless I think it accurate to say that, between 1880 and 1920, something really new occurred in American Protestantism.

Certainly there was no lack of social forces conducive to change. The Civil War had called nationhood into question. Immigrants, many of whom were not Protestant, were coming in droves. Factories were being built, and millions were moving out of rural settings into cities. America was becoming a world power. Public schools were distributing the products of the Enlightenment to more and more people, as evolution and textual analysis became part of everyday intellectual baggage; and higher education grew increasingly secular. Labor was organizing, and the vicissitudes of a capitalist economy were becoming evermore apparent.

The question is how to describe Protestantism's response to these social forces. As Henry May said: "In 1876 Protestantism presented a massive, almost unbroken front in its defense of the social status quo. Two decades later social criticism had penetrated deeply into each major church" (1949, p. 91).

But more than criticism of the social status quo was involved. Martin Marty writes:

> From the 1880s to World War I the mainline Protestants saw much of their intellectual leadership adopt various versions of the new theology and much of their reformist passion shaped into a new social gospel. Biblical criticism, evolutionary thought, and modern secular philosophy were absorbed into the liberal Protestant patterns . (1970, p. 211)

In other words, Protestantism was recognizing not just the existence of social problems in need of correction but also the existence of standards lying outside of Protestantism itself, standards by which these problems, and efforts to solve them, would be judged.

Robert Handy is correct, therefore, in calling this period the breakup of the "Protestant era." Pre-Revolutionary legal efforts to make America a "Christian nation" had failed, but Protestantism bounced back with a voluntary plan that, through much of the nineteenth century, worked to make this nonetheless a "Protestant nation." But events late in the century began an erosion process that went on for the next several decades. This "second disestablishment," as Handy calls it, resulted in profound changes in the relationship between Protestantism and the surrounding society.

Of course, many were unhappy with the adjustments Protestantism was making. To put it mildly, there was no lack of theological debate during these years of transition. Through it all, however, was the implicit issue of whether America would remain a Protestant nation. As Princeton theologian, George Patton, put it in 1897:

> Let us be honest with ourselves. Let us face the question whether Christianity is a supernatural religion or not, whether it is from heaven or of men, whether it is the absolute religion or simply the purest form of religion that has yet appeared. . . . [I]f we believe the latter, let us give up the old terminology and the old method of defending the faith. And when we have given up the God-man Christ Jesus, and the miracles He wrought, and His resurrection from the dead, and His atonement for sin, then . . . let us pause and ask . . . whether we are still Christians. (quoted in Hutchison, 1976, p. 204)

To most American religious leaders the answer, by 1920, was clear: No, we are not still Christians, at least not in the same sense Americans were before 1880. Not just new doctrines but new relationships— new social structures, if you will—are needed, they said, if Protestantism is to remain a force in American life. The conservatives' alleged choice between the Christian orthodoxy of the nineteenth century and no Christianity at all was understood by the liberals as a choice between a believable Christianity and no *religion* at all (Hutchison, 1976, p. 258). Just as early nineteenth century Protestants woke up to the inevitability of a voluntary church, so early twentieth century Protestants woke up to the inevitability of pluralism, the authority of science, and the realities of an urbanized, capitalistic society.[1]

The consequences of this new awareness were vast, only two of which will I touch on here: (1) the altered relationship between Protestant churches and the domestic political agenda, and (2) a failure of nerve in the foreign mission field.

TWENTIETH-CENTURY PROTESTANTISM AND DOMESTIC KINGDOM BUILDING

Protestantism after 1880 found it had taken a giant step in the inner-worldly ascetic direction, reflected most clearly in the changing role of millenialism. At least implicitly, Protestants until the Civil War assumed the Second Coming would come magically, following some cataclysm. Inspired by such leaders as Washington Gladden and Walter Rauschenbusch, however, churches began working actively to assist in the Kingdom's arrival. The founding of the Federal Council of Churches in 1908 was the organizational achievement in this direction, and almost as a first act it adopted the "Social Creed of the Churches" (Miller, 1958, pp. 220-221).

This inner-worldly ascetic step must, however, be seen in proper perspective. It was not simply a recognition that the world is filled with evil needing correction, nor was it simply a naive optimism that human effort could correct evil. Neo-orthodoxy a few decades later tried to pin such charges on the Social Gospelers, and superficially they were accurate charges. But much more profound was the underlying change in soteriology. People now would take responsibility for the salvation of all of society. As Donald Meyer puts it: "Rauschenbusch . . . allowed himself to believe in history" (1960, p. 16). But not just Rauschenbusch; all Social Gospelers. And not just Social Gospelers; most Protestant leaders, the Niebuhr brothers included. This world was recognized as the only world in which human action could meaningfully occur, and like it or not, with hope or with despair, people were called on to act on the stage of history. And this meant—if one acted responsibly in a religiously plural setting—justifying one's actions not by revealed, otherworldly, or otherwise private criteria (even if one claimed such criteria as inspiration) but by the criteria of a secular, humanistic society.

Thus, when Rauschenbusch wrote of the church: "She does not exist for her own sake; she is simply a working organization to create the Christian life in individuals and the kingdom of God in human society" (1907, p. 185), he was inviting a consensual definition of "Christian life" and "kingdom of God." He was, to put it another way, announcing an eagerness to work with non-Christians to achieve a goal they mutually recognized though they might call it by different names. As Handy remarks: "The kingdom idea was in many respects a spiritualized and idealized restatement of the search for a specifically Christian society [but] in an age of freedom and progress" (1971, p. 101). To put it yet another way, the church would now do its work in this world, according to worldly standards, and the channels through which it worked would be judged by their effectiveness, not by their fidelity to some doctrine. Although one may question Henry May's assertion that the Social Gospel influenced the "progressivism" of Theodore Roosevelt,

Robert LaFollette, Woodrow Wilson, and FDR (1949, pp. 204-234), there is no disputing that official Protestantism came to share the political criteria—and eventually the political agenda—of secular parties. For it to do anything else would have been to be irrelevant in a post-Protestant society.

What we observe in this change after the 1880s is Protestantism's growing awareness that it no longer set the moral agenda for the nation. Prohibition was probably the last expression of the earlier outlook, but, as is now recognized, Prohibition's success depended on a temporary coalition that included many groups for whom alcohol was not the chief enemy. Granted, many Social Gospelers who applauded labor unions, welfare programs, and a progressive income tax still balked at FDR and the New Deal because of the alcohol issue. But once the awareness was complete enough, once Protestant leaders saw what the realistic choices were, they made a kind of peace with politics, generally the Democratic Party. As Robert M. Miller noted: "The New Deal program received almost unfailing support from the Federal Council. . . . the Roosevelt program did approximate the political equivalent of the Council's social ideals" (1958, pp. 88-89). Of course, individual church members, then as now, were among the chief detractors of the New Deal. Even some denominations were reluctant to depart from the Republican Party, the party that for almost a century had been the conduit through which Protestantism had helped exercise power. Through the 1920s and 1930s, the magazines of these denominations exhibit this ambivalent character as they espouse various social programs on the one hand, while on the other hand expressing distrust of the Democratic Party, made up as it was of Catholics, Jews, machine politicians, and of course "wets."[2]

There was also the problem of war. The liberal tendency pushing Protestants toward support of government social programs was also pushing them toward pacifism and isolation. World War I was an especially difficult event for those progressives to digest.

In this postwar period of liberal confusion and despair Reinhold Niebuhr rose to prominence, bringing the counsel of realism: No program of human devising is capable of redeeming the world, he said. War is an acceptable, even necessary, tactic if the evil it is designed to destroy is greater than the evil war itself represents. The chief mistake Christians make, especially Christians who are heirs to the nineteenth century Protestant era, is to believe God's will is to be found in history, to believe that a religion taking its goals from the surrounding society is authentic religion. Such beliefs, Niebuhr said, are mere "culture religion," which, knowing "no God who transcends all cultures and civilizations . . . therefore identifies God with the highest culture it knows" (1938, p. 9).

The weakness of the Niebuhrian position was obvious, however. It was one thing to hold to a neo-orthodoxy that was uncompromising in its relations with culture; it was quite another to make any claims in the name of that neo-orthodoxy if one were simultaneously: (1) committed to the ideal of religious pluralism, and (2) convinced that action in this world is obligatory. Neo-orthodoxy in America therefore left Protestants chastised for being naively optimistic, but, as Benton Johnson reminded us (1982), it otherwise did nothing to improve on liberal Protestantism's efforts to grapple with real social problems. On this score, neo-orthodoxy suffered the same fate as liberalism; it played according to the rules and with the agenda set by others, or it did not play at all. Protestantism by now had no special power of its own.

So vividly did neo-orthodoxy follow this same course that I will take a few more moments to illustrate with material that might otherwise be relegated to a footnote. In 1935 Niebuhr founded the journal *Radical Religion* and was its editor for several years. Among other themes prominent in its pages was the indictment of culture religion, especially as manifested in any "American Dream," including high hopes for New Deal legislation. Many of Roosevelt's programs, Niebuhr thought, were facades for "predatory interests." One of the spokesmen for this point of view was Richard W. Day, at the time a priest at All Angels Episcopal Church in New York City and a regular contributor to *Radical Religion*.

In 1938, however, Day wrote an essay entitled "American Dream Resurgent." It appeared in the winter issue of the journal, no doubt with Niebuhr's editorial approval. "A new alignment of political thinking is taking place among radicals, liberals and progressives in America," Day wrote. "The New Deal has had telling effect. . . . Roosevelt and his program seem to be going somewhere" (1938, p. 16).

So far, so good. Faced with two imperfect options, even the neoorthodox must make choices. The telling point comes in Day's subsequent argument, where he allowed himself to express the belief that, in "going somewhere," Roosevelt's program is approximating "the American Dream." He is still aware, he says, of the dangers of mistaking the American Dream (a culture religion) for authentic religion, but

> in spite of that, an appeal must be made to the American
> Dream. In its political and economic aspects, every attempt
> must be made to clarify it, showing what is feasible and desir-
> able in our present situation. . . . It is impossible to say how
> much in the culture religion of the American Dream is Christian
> and how much is idolatrous; but there is some Christianity in
> it. . . . The strength which even a false hope generates can be
> used for divine purposes. (Day, 1938, p. 21)

Like Rauschenbusch before them, the neo-orthodox also had allowed
themselves to believe in history.

But how could it have been otherwise? All magic had been relinquished by Protestantism a generation or two before when it recognized it had no special claim in setting the moral agenda. Yet it still
regarded this world as an appropriate arena for action. Because neo-
orthodoxy repudiated neither of these propositions, it was left with
having to believe in the merits of its positions not because they were
"Christian" but because they met certain standards whether or not they
were Christian.[3]

Protestantism, in other words, had entered the world to such a
degree that the boundary between it and any secular design for the
good society was hard to find. Its special link with the exercise of power
in America was dissolved to the point where an identifiable Protestant
twentieth century had disappeared.

FAILURE OF NERVE IN FOREIGN MISSIONS

On the international scene, too, mainline Protestantism has played a
diminishing role in this century, at least since the 1920s. Through most
of the nineteenth century, Protestant missionaries, whether to American
Indians, Hawaii, the Levant, or East Asia had a clear goal: to convert
pagans into Christians. As late as the Boxer Rebellion in 1900, missionaries in China were thus of the mind that a "punitive expedition should
go to Pao Ting and destroy the city." Missionaries, said another of them,
"are the vanguard of Western civilization." Thus it is proper "to make
converts in a country like China," even "if the outcome is to be trouble
and perhaps war" (Miller, 1974, pp. 274, 280). A Methodist bishop
declared it "worth any cost in bloodshed if we can make millions of
Chinese true and intelligent Christians" (Schlesinger, Jr., 1974, p. 358).

With the rise of Protestant liberalism and the shift from pre- to postmillenialism, however, such foreign mission thinking was revised. And surprisingly, the initial impact of this revision was a tremendous surge in missionary activity. At least three factors were at play. First, about this time many foreign governments actively sought missionaries from America, believing that they brought cultural and economic progress (Hutchison, 1976, p. 260). Second, the developing split between modernists and conservatives did not lead in the foreign field to the same antagonisms it did domestically, so that people like John R. Mott and Sherwood Eddy could appeal simultaneously to both sides. Third, and perhaps most important, the giant inner-worldly ascetic step Protestantism took after 1880 meant new energies were released toward the goal of "building the Kingdom on earth." The Student Volunteer Movement, a device for recruiting college students into the missionary enterprise, blossomed through its summer conferences, reaching a peak of 2700 recruits in 1920 (Handy, 1971, p. 201). "Evangelizing the world in this generation" became the slogan to express the incredible optimism early twentieth-century Protestantism felt about its work in foreign fields. From fewer than 1000 in 1890, North American missionary personnel rose ninefold by 1915, and passed the 11,000 mark in 1925 (Hogg, 1977).

After this initial burst in missionary activity, however, Protestantism faced a failure of nerve abroad just as it did at home. Surely World War I contributed to the crisis, calling into question the churches' effectiveness in "Christianizing" the world. More important, doubt arose over the very meaning of *Christian*. One National Council spokesman expressed in 1920 what many were thinking: "The so-called Christian nations are approaching moral and spiritual bankruptcy" (quoted in Handy, 1971, p. 196). From a period early in the century, then, a period with little reason to doubt the superiority of the Protestant version of Christianity, American Protestant leaders rather suddenly came to question the whole mission enterprise. No better evidence for this failure of nerve exists than the 1932 publication of *Re-thinking Missions*, a National Council report issued under the direction of Harvard philosopher William Ernest Hocking. The report called not only for an end to sectarian competition in the mission field but also urged cooperation with non-Christians, to the end that concern for indigenous cultures be fostered and self-determination replace missionary influence.

It perhaps does not matter that this report was heavily criticized, because it was recommending the inevitable anyway. Add the Depression, plus the growing issues of pacifism and interventionism as World War II, Korea, and Vietnam came and went, and one can understand the radical decline in missionaries supported by mainline Protestant denominations in recent decades. From 11,000 in 1925, the figure dropped to 8,000 in 1952, 6,000 in 1970, and 3,000 in 1976. The decline continues.

As important as sheer mechanical problems like war might have been, however, such a precipitous drop must be understood socially as well. American mainline denominations had lost their conviction that *as Christians* they had much to offer. As Robert Handy said, foreign missions were rooted in the evangelical Protestantism coming out of the nineteenth century. When that viewpoint ceased to be the primary definer of cultural values and behavior patterns, the institutions that viewpoint helped create eventually eroded. From 2,700 recruits in 1920, the Student Volunteer Movement signed a mere 252 in 1928 (Handy, 1971, p. 201). As successive generations of missionaries retired, in other words, few were available as replacements. One can find many consequences of American missionary activity—some of them enormously important, as John Fairbank has argued (1974)—but they came about chiefly as the result of pre-1920s goals and inspiration. One does not find comparable Protestant foreign missions later in the twentieth century.

THE RESURGENCE OF CONSERVATIVE PROTESTANTISM

If mainline Protestantism began losing its foreign mission nerve around 1920, the same can hardly be said of other Protestants. Table 1.1 shows the number of North American Protestant missionary personnel, for selected years, according to their denominational sponsorship.

Although missionaries sponsored by members of the National Council were declining from 11,000 in 1925 to 3,000 in 1976, nonmember bodies were increasing their missionaries from 2,500 to 30,000. Put another way, denominations united in the National Council sponsored 81 percent of the Protestant missionaries in 1925; they sponsored 9 percent in 1976, 7 percent in 1985 (Hogg,1977; Dayton, 1986). By as early as 1938, Littell claimed, it was evident that "the main portion of finance and personnel going into the expansion of Christianity in new fields

TABLE 1.1

North American Protestant Missionary Personnel
(of which about 10% are Canadian)

Sponsor	1890	1915	1925	1952	1960	1970	1973	1976
Denominations belonging to NCCC[a]	934	9,072	11,020	7,937	8,213	6,199	4,013	3,105
NCCC affiliated but not belonging[b]				2,439	2,111	3,258	2,908	2,234
All others[c]			2,588	8,160	19,056	25,003	28,149	30,119
Total	934	9,072	13,608	18,536	29,380	34,460	35,070	35,458

[a] Inasmuch as the National Council (earlier, the Federal Council) did not form until 1908, the first figure in this row is technically mislabeled.

[b] The largest of these sponsors are Seventh Day Adventist, Missouri Synod Lutheran, and American Lutheran Church.

[c] The largest of these sponsors are Southern Baptist and Wycliffe Bible Translators.

SOURCE: W. Richie Hogg, "The Role of American Protestantism in World Mission," in R. P. Beaver, ed., *American Missions in Bicentennial Perspective.* Adapted from Tables III and VI.

was coming from the Free Churches. . . . from smaller fundamentalistic and pentecostal groups" (Littell, 1971, p. 130). The reasons for this decline among mainline Protestant bodies have just been reviewed. What is now to be asked is why Protestants outside of the mainline—Protestants we have so far lumped together as conservative—have followed a markedly different course.

The American religious movement that includes what we now call millenarian, evangelical, or fundamentalist groups had its proximate origins in the 1870s. Before this time, after all, the movement was hardly distinguishable from Protestant orthodoxy. From about 1880 to about 1920, however, conservative Protestantism—it remained several different submovements, each with its own special item on a fairly common agenda—arose as a minority party opposed to the theological adaptations being made by others. It was, in other words, a movement rooted in theology. Its leaders were drawn in part from Episcopal, Presbyterian, and Baptist clergy in good standing, and its strength lay among the bourgeoisie of the Northern cities (Sandeen, 1970; Marsden, 1980). Whether the primary concern was the Second Coming, biblical inerrancy, Genesis vs. evolution, or recognition of the Holy Spirit, conservatives before 1920 were collectively alarmed at what was happening to *Protestantism*. What bothered them was not economics, politics, and social welfare so much as cosmology, ontology, and teleology. They correctly perceived the ebbing away of the "Protestant Era," and they tried to staunch it.

By the 1920s, however, it was clear they had failed. America was no longer a "Christian" nation; the Bible had lost its authority, and the church had lost control of education. These facts are what made the Scopes trial of 1925 so symbolic. What had for several decades been a middle-class movement, as much within as alongside the major denominations, was now changing in leadership and in the social bases of its support. It was divorcing from mainline Protestantism.

But not just mainline Protestantism; the conservative movement was also at odds with the direction America was moving. Having lost the theological battle in mainline churches, conservatives turned their attention to cultural matters and necessarily became political as well. The teaching of evolution vs. creation in the schools ceased to be simply a dispute about Genesis among persons sharing a Christian culture and became instead an issue of the imminent collapse of a misguided civilization.[4] Prohibition may have been the last issue on which these disputants agreed, but, as we saw, even that coalition broke down in the 1930s.

Within a few years there came into existence an elaborate net-work of parallel institutions to counteract the collapse: Bible schools and mission organizations, journals of opinions and publishing houses, new denominations and innovative ministries to youth. Conservative Protestantism exploited radio—and then TV—in ways mainline churches have yet to duplicate. It is no exaggeration to call the result a *folk religion*, perhaps—a religion much practiced by people but little recognized in the formal culture. Certainly the institutions of this folk religion were hardly noticed by majoritarian culture. Its books went unreviewed by the secular press, its radio shows remained local, and its schools showed little concern for national accreditation. It comes as a bit of a shock to realize, for example, that Hal Lindsey's *The Late Great Planet Earth* was the best-selling nonfiction work of the entire decade of the 1970s.

Surely the cadre of sympathetic followers who served, and in turn were served by, this institutional network is a crucial ingredient in the conservative resurgence in the current day, but by itself this cadre explains little. If the sentiment has been there for over half a century, what happened in recent years to activate it, give it voice, strength, and visibility.

Two answers might be offered, both implied in the analysis so far. One answer helps explain the strident political tone found in some present-day Conservative Protestants. The other answer does more to explain the popularity of a Conservative Protestantism that remains largely nonpolitical.

The first answer is that, in becoming political since the 1920s, conservative Protestantism had to wait only until the forces of modernity became also the forces leading to oblivion—to Armageddon, if you will. During the Depression, World War II, the era of Sputnick, Keynesian adjustments, and Great Society programs, modernity was the path of hope for most Americans. Those who bemoaned the consequences of weakened family, neighborhood, school, church, and community were dismissed as mere alarmists. By the 1970s, however, even some erst-while liberals had joined in alarm at the breakdown in these traditional authority structures. How reasonable it was, therefore, that the mes-sage being preached by conservative religious leaders now resonated through a wider audience and the mass media. The Tri-lateral Com-mission, the Council on Foreign Affairs, and regulatory agencies such as Health and Human Services would join the Supreme Court and Com-munist Russia as forces of darkness. Not just the outlawing of school prayers but the London price of gold, the MX missile, and ERA would become Christian issues.

The other answer helps explain why the conservative Protestantism enjoying renewed vigor has nevertheless remained largely nonpolitical. This answer involves the "cure of souls." Not only did mainline Protestantism tend to lose out on this score after 1920, but so also did its conservative counterpart muscle into that territory. To be sure, the concern for peace of mind and personal tranquility is not new to the conservative movement (Marsden, 1980, p. 75). But what was surely of little concern to conservatives between 1880 and 1920 had, by the 1950s and especially the 1970s, become a significant part of that movement's message. *Publishers Weekly* claims that the best-selling religious titles today are "experience-oriented, life-centered, and Bible-based" (Quebedeaux, 1982, p. 48). Positive Thinking, in other words, is at least as popular as Armageddon, as suggested by titles such as *The Christian Mother Goose* and *God's Answer to Fat: Lose It*. Billy Graham combined with Norman Vincent Peale, a merger in fact in 1957, although as Richard Quebedeaux remarks, "It took another two decades for the content and method of revivalistic Christianity and New Thought to blend together at the grass-roots" (1982, p. 82; see also Hunter, 1983).

It is this last answer, it seems to me, that best explains how conservative Protestantism can be at once political, popular, and yet remain outrageously eccentric theologically. Giving utterance to antiintellectual, antidemocratic, and antimodern sentiments, the conservative then adds the implicit, "But only for me, of course. You may believe what you like." The political directives perceived by some, in other words, are as foreign and irrelevant to the majority of religious conservatives as civil rights, nuclear disarmament, and corporate investment in South Africa are to the majority of religious liberals. I have no doubt that conservative leaders who would force the teaching of creation or bomb Godless Russia are serious. But their followers, I suspect, are not. Stacey and Shupe, for example, who studied this precise point report: "our data . . . suggest that viewers and listeners are attracted to the electronic church by its religious messages, and any political . . . dimension associated with those messages is either 'filtered out' (i.e., ignored) or is of fairly low importance to the audiences" (1982). Moral Majoritarians watched the "jiggle" shows on TV in the same proportions as the rest of the public. If necessary, they perhaps justified watching the Dallas Cowboy cheerleaders because Roger Staubach was a born-again quarterback. The forces of modernity are real, after all, however depraved their products. Maybe, therefore, if one is provided a means of expressing alarm, plus some techniques for adjusting to the depravity one is alarmed about, that is all one asks.[5] In this connection, it is wise to recognize how few social proposals of the New Christian Right have been enacted legislatively: not the ban on abortions, nor the return to school prayers, nor the tax exemption for private segregated schools, nor the measure to restrict school busing, nor the tuition tax credit. Surely Congress in the 1980s and President Reagan were as congenial to such proposals as America is likely to see. But these proposals run counter to cultural forces not easily reversed. By contrast, declaring oneself "born again" or preferring conservative over liberal offerings from the religious cafeteria do not, in any similar sense, encounter such opposition. (It is possible that a changing judicial climate may accomplish what legislative efforts have not.)

CONCLUSION

There is no gainsaying Conservative Protestantism enjoys a renewed vitality in the present day. One might therefore imagine mainline, Liberal Protestantism to be its antagonist; but it is not. Although ostensibly a religious movement, today's Conservative Protestantism is better described as a folk religion with a political wing. Put another way, despite the rhetoric and the undoubted origins in a turn-of-the-century theological controversy, the movement today is not an effort to renew that controversy. It is rather one part in the struggle over the American cultural agenda.

Not liberal theology, then, but what conservatives call "secular humanism" is the real target; and National Council churches reflect but do not create secular humanism any more than they create the American political agenda. One can search for a Protestant twentieth century in America, therefore, but not find it. Only if Conservative Protestantism should win the day—a remote possibility at best, it seems to me—is there even a chance anything distinctively Christian in label will remain in our political life.

Nor is this unexpected. In 1820, Daniel Webster declared, "Whatever makes men good Christians, makes them good citizens," a sentiment John Adams heartily endorsed, as did most other national leaders, no doubt. But Webster was not aware of the variety of Christians, and the variety of non-Christians, America was to become. Nor could he anticipate how science and scholarship would challenge the role of the Bible or how urban industrial society would demand universalism. A century later many Americans had faced these issues, and new conclusions had been drawn. "Whatever makes good citizens," one of these conclusions might be paraphrased, "permits good Christians—and others—to exist." Of course, the result *sounds* like mere secular humanism, but only to those whose Christianity got stuck in the nineteenth century. The fact is, Protestantism lost sovereignty, and Liberal Protestantism lost centrality as well. Conservative Protestantism, in regaining visibility, may be said to have increased in centrality since 1950, but such a change should not be mistaken as regained sovereignty. We explore this point more carefully in the next chapter.

2

The Moral Majority and All That: The Curious Path of Conservative Protestantism

Whether religion is judged to be conservative depends less on its doctrines than on its relationship to society. Because Conservative Protestantism in America in the 1980s was not always conservative, the task of this essay—to trace its curious path and thus give contextual meaning to the movement that became popularly known as the Moral Majority—is really to track its transmutations. Although we could start even earlier, then, we choose to begin this story in the first decades of the nineteenth century.

THE EARLY NINETEENTH CENTURY

For some years early in the nineteenth century, the American states and frontier were swept by a series of religious revivals generally labeled the *Second Great Awakening*. The major residue of these revivals was what we might call the voluntary church syndrome, a religious pattern we know variously as the separation of church and state, religious freedom, the competitiveness and commercialization of religious organizations, and the privatization of faith. Ironically, the way was being paved for a decrease in both the sovereignty and centrality of religion. Though not uniquely Protestant, this voluntary church syndrome was felt first and most deeply in Protestantism.

One reason was because this voluntary religious pattern had greater theological warrant in Protestantism than it did in Catholicism or Judaism. Catholic theology stressed the role of liturgy, priest, and church; Judaism, the role of community and ritual law. But Protestants were, so to speak, already theologically prepared to be told that salvation was their own responsibility, that internal spirituality was the measure of a Christian, and that inner light should shine out in the form of upright behavior.

The Second Great Awakening thus went far in enabling individualistic evangelicalism to become the dominant religious perspective in America. Clergy and church gained in popularity even as they lost in power; formally, that is, religion declined, even if informally its influence spread. Many features of organized life Americans take now for granted—for example, hospitals, publishing firms, newspapers and magazines, and colleges—owe their origins to the religious enthusiasm of Protestant Christians intent on evangelizing society in the nineteenth century.

This evangelical Protestantism was hardly conservative, therefore, at least not *religiously* conservative, for it was in fact a new development, a departure from Puritan orthodoxy. It was a religion that capitalized on the growing sense of individualism even as it exalted social responsibility. A society in the throes of establishing democracy—of extending the vote and elevating the commoner, of demolishing hereditary privilege and holding out the promise of success for all, of broadening liberties while relying on self-control—such a society could hardly ask for a more compatible religion. Evangelicalism rather quickly became the dominant religious outlook, therefore, and not just among Protestants.

That this outlook had a strong reformist element is well known, abolition being its most visible early expression. Less dramatic but no doubt more widespread, however, was the element in evangelicalism that contributed to its subsequent conservatism: the "paradoxical combination of libertarianism and traditionalism."[1] Developing throughout the century along with the American nation, this element became as close to an "established" theology, with a parallel moral consensus, as America will ever know. In the nineteenth century it motivated missionaries to build schools and cover native breasts. It encouraged capitalists to build factories and hedge their investments with philanthropy. It exalted rural and small town ideals, saturating America with the idea that people should be free to do pretty much as they like, as long as they look out for themselves . . . and, of course, behave. American evangelical Protestantism, it might be said, provided a creed that, even today, can stir Americans to action.

AT THE TURN OF THE CENTURY

In due time, of course, social forces greatly challenged this creed; views that made sense in the context of farm, small town, and neighborhood were hard to sustain in the city, factory, and university. In these latter places the forces of modernity had to be confronted. Because persons differed in their closeness to modernity, however, they also differed in · their responses to it.

Sometime after the Civil War, and for the next several decades, there developed within Protestantism two camps regarding this question of modernity and just how to contend with it. As Peter Berger reminded us,[2] then as now the religious choices were basically two: accommodate religion to worldly circumstances, meeting changes with all available resources, *or* hold firm to the religious convictions, insisting that worldly changes do not alter supernatural truths. The first choice created "liberals," the second "conservatives." The evangelicalism that had been mainline evangelicalism through most of the nineteenth century thus became Conservative Protestantism by 1920, not so much because its tenets changed but because the surrounding world changed, and many Protestants not only did not change with it but also elaborated a theology as to why they should not change. About this time, indeed, there appeared a series of pamphlets proclaiming the "fundamentals" of Christian doctrine, from which came the label *Fundamentalist*, a title used by friend and foe alike. Evangelicalism was still firmly entrenched in some sectors, but now it was defensive, locked in a struggle with its accommodative counterpart over control of Protestant institutions in America: local churches certainly, but more strategically the seminaries, church-related colleges, denominational headquarters, the church media, and thus the "public" face of Protestantism.

Conservatism lost that struggle, with the Scopes trial of 1925 the publicized scene of surrender. The conservative troops did not dissolve and fade away, of course, but they were now weakened in leadership and infrastructure. Their "established" status had all but disappeared, to be taken over by the hated enemies they called, with justification, *modernists*.

What exactly was the battle about? The forces of modernity over which Protestantism split, may be conveniently grouped into three areas: (1) immigration, especially of Roman Catholics, thus calling into question Protestant hegemony; (2) industrialization, especially in urban centers, thus revealing the need for new kinds of social ministries; and (3) education, especially in the form of Darwinism and biblical higher criticism, thus evoking new understanding of the Scriptures. Generally speaking, liberal Protestants saw the need to accommodate in all three of those areas; what had been conventional behavior and thought in the pulpit, seminary, and denominational office became, in little more than one generation, outmoded and disreputable—at least to the vast majority of Protestants occupying pulpits, seminaries, and denominational offices. (As we shall see later, the change was by no means so swift or so widespread among Protestants in the pews.)[3]

Theologically another difference developed between the two camps: liberals became explicitly "postmillenial" in outlook, meaning that Christ's return awaits human effort and success in bringing about the Kingdom on earth. Many conservatives absorbed and upheld the opposing "premillenial" view: that things will get worse before Christ comes again to reign for a thousand years, and no human agency can influence the outcome; the most that persons can do is repent, get saved, and await the "rapture."

Actually premillialism was only one of several theological tributaries coming out of the past to make up the Conservative Protestant stream. Two others of importance were Reformed or Calvinist orthodoxy and holiness teaching. As different as these three were from each other, however, they share the label *conservative* because all three, in Berger's words, "refused to accommodate themselves . . . and continued to profess the old objectivities as much as possible as if nothing had happened."[4]

FROM THE 1920s TO THE 1960s

The struggle over modernity was thus won by the liberal accommodationists, and they now controlled the so-called mainline churches. Evangelical Protestants, now Conservative, either grew silent and disaffected in the pews of those mainline churches (and this was the case for many) or else they found new, oftentimes "nondenominational," churches. And not just churches but Bible schools, colleges, radio (and then TV) ministries, publishing houses, and journals as well; that is, there developed new leadership and new infrastructure. Conservative Protestants did not forego the public arena altogether—for example, between 1921 and 1929, thirty-seven antievolution bills were introduced in twenty state legislatures[5]—but, having lost the theological war for control of the ecclesiastical mainstream, Conservatives essentially "submerged" from public life and instead turned inward. Their earlier objections on theological grounds to Catholicism, Darwinism, and higher criticism did not exactly disappear, but neither did the warfare continue. Instead, they regrouped and, as it turns out, prepared behind the scenes for a new kind of battle.

Meanwhile, Liberal Protestantism accommodated mightily. Optimistic in its adjustments to secular forces, it took as its goal the evangelization of the world in one generation. It was also prepared to end all wars and solve all social problems. When warfare and economic depression interfered, a flirtation with neo-orthodoxy ensued, but neo-orthodoxy's impact was primarily to temper the optimism, not reverse Liberalism's worldly accommodation.

When mainline denominations thus cooperated in waging World War II, and this was followed by the ecclesiastical bull market of the late 1950s, the overlap of Liberal Protestantism with modern, liberal culture was nearly complete. Churches absorbed the New Deal ethic, along with the belief that government agencies *are* the proper way, after all, to address social problems. Ecumenism was espoused, denominational loyalty becoming simply a matter of stylistic liturgical preference. Civil rights, world peace, redistributed wealth, and control of nuclear arms became other planks in liberal Protestantism's agenda.

Of course, not everyone in the liberal denominations concurred with this agenda. Especially among many lay people, the churches' pursuit of "social Christianity" at the expense of "the Gospel" caused unhappiness. That is to say, even if some kind of theological peace had been achieved, the old "paradoxical combination" of libertarianism and traditionalism could generate unhappiness on moral grounds. People who may not really have cared about the turn-of-the-century *theological* battle lost by conservative Protestantism could nevertheless still care deeply about nineteenth century *moral* formulations that were once expressed in those theological terms. Such people were, so to speak, political or cultural conservatives who had no respectable political or cultural channels for expressing their unease. For them, therefore, conservative religion became their outlet.

THE CURRENT SCENE

Americans have in their midst, then, a sizeable, visible, and vocal set of people—roughly identifiable as Conservative Protestants—whose nineteenth century pedigree is not conservative at all. Many are found in mainline denominations, but many more have long since gone elsewhere. They and their predecessors, having chosen not to engage and address the forces of modern social life, retrenched through most of the twentieth century, only to burst now onto the national scene, via the media and political arena, espousing a religious viewpoint common enough 100 years ago but long ago judged naive by most literate Americans.

Theologically that viewpoint is still naive, as pathetic attempts to defend biblical literalism, especially creationism, illustrate.[6] It is not that such beliefs are no longer held by many; they clearly are and have been all along. But for more than half a century, people holding those beliefs kept silent in public, and now they are noisy. We can ask why the curious path of conservative Protestantism has taken this direction.

Actually that issue, as the discussion to now would suggest, translates into two questions: Why has evangelical Protestantism surged in visible popularity since the 1970s? And why has it taken such a political turn? The remainder of this essay will be devoted to these two questions, against the backdrop of the brief history just covered.

THE CURRENT POPULARITY OF CONSERVATIVE PROTESTANTISM

The first thing to be said about Conservative Protestantism's current popularity is that even more important than new *membership* in the movement is the new *notoriety* the movement has received in recent years. Conservative Protestants, in other words, did not disappear after 1920, only to reappear in the 1970s. Rather, social scientists and the mass media "discovered" them, even as they were showing renewed signs of strength,[7] and some were even desiring public attention.

A second observation thus has to do with the facilities available to conservative Protestants since the 1970s that were not readily available before. Among these, television no doubt ranks supreme, for it was televangelists who first discovered the potential of slick broadcasting. Mainline denominations had long helped fill those "public service" hours, on radio as well as television, but as a service, not in the aggressive, entrepreneurial manner of the 1980s' Jerry Falwell, Robert Schuller, Jimmy Swaggart, et al.[8] Related is the investment of several decades of training new leaders, establishing networks of communication, and developing its own "public" face. Billy Graham stands out here, of course, as no one can match his four decades of spokemanship at many levels, from personal crusade to TV to book writing to counseling Presidents. When the time was "ripe," in other words, conservative Protestantism was prepared through its many, many organizations to capitalize on its ripened opportunities.

But what made the time "ripe"? More specifically, what made Evangelical Protestantism an attractive response to events in the 1970s? James Hunter, in his splendid analysis, *American Evangelicals*, provides the single most important clue. It is true, he points out, that Conservative Protestants lost the *theological* battle after 1920, but their *moral viewpoint* was shared at the time by most Americans; and this moral viewpoint continued to be the dominant conventional viewpoint until the 1960s.[9] At that time in the United States, this long-term moral consensus was severely challenged. It was one thing to lose theological control of the major denominations, in other words, but it was quite another to see all of American culture threatening to deviate from the "paradoxical combination" of libertarianism and traditionalism: the conventionality inherited from the nineteenth century.

In effect, the Democratic Party platform after 1932 must have seemed to many to advocate just that, but no doubt the countercultural-ists of the 1960s were symbolically bigger offenders. Similarly profound reverberations must have been brought on by the women's movement and by affirmative action on behalf of blacks, homosexuals, unmarried mothers, and so on. Upsetting also were court decisions declaring abortion to be right and school prayer wrong.[10] Although the experience of "moral crisis" alone is not sufficient to explain the outpouring of evangelical fervor beginning in the 1970s, then, certainly that sense of crisis, when directed by sophisticated leaders who are themselves interconnected and alert to the mass media, was a crucial element.

But even more can be said. The Vietnam war proved futile as military strategy but all too convincing as evidence that cold war tensions are not amenable to simple-minded solutions. If conventional warfare is no longer feasible, and nuclear confrontation is indeed unthinkable, then the way is open to invent (or, in this case, reinvent) a scenario wherein at least good guys and bad guys can be identified. The premillenialist vision serves nicely in this regard.[11]

Another factor to be mentioned is a psychological change, purportedly widespread, but one on which conservative Protestantism could capitalize in a novel way. This has been to join evangelical religion with so-called new thought: putting together Billy Graham and Norman Vincent Peale, as Richard Quebedeaux so felicitously recounts it.[12] When the world seems out of control in almost every other respect, accepting Christ as one's "personal" savior may provide not only a certain comfort but also a warrant for not worrying whether the world, too, is still redeemable.

Yet another factor helping to explain why conservative Protestantism blossomed in popularity in the 1970s is the halt to economic growth, the retracting of an economy that had been chiefly expanding for decades. This factor has had impact throughout the social structure, of course, but if government programs to enhance life had to be curtailed, if civil rights (of criminals, for example) were going to be restricted, then a certain repose might be derived from seeing these not as failures of an idealistic agenda but as ideologically demanded. In a book that is otherwise curiously argued, Jeremy Rifkin points out how compatible was accommodative, optimistic Protestantism with economic expansionism.[13] If, then, such expansion has ceased, if exploitation of the world's resources is leveling off, it is understandable that the seductive theology accompanying expansion would also experience difficulty. Where Rifkin errs is in seeing evangelicalism as a "solution" rather than a response to this no-growth situation, and thus he fails to note its reactionary character. It is, after all, conservatives, not liberals, who defend nuclear power plants, off-shore oil drilling, the harvesting of redwoods, acid rain, and so forth.

In sum, to a significant degree, conservative Protestantism has become a refuge for those Americans who, faced with a crisis brought on by a sharp escalation in the moral agonies associated with modern life, choose not to accommodate but persist in defining those agonies in once-common ways. Though for many these definitions are theological, the crisis evoking them is not doctrinal so much as it is political or cultural. Evangelical language, so to speak, is but a convenient way to express one view of this crisis. As Hunter's analysis shows, the single strongest correlate of an evangelical outlook today is distance from modern social life; that is, the low level of education, rural residence, occupation unrelated to high technology, and so on.[14]

THE POLITICAL INVOLVEMENT OF CONSERVATIVE PROTESTANTISM

If a surge in the popularity of Conservative Protestantism can thus be explained with reference to the agonies associated with modern life, what explains its distinct—and, since the 1920s, unusual—political turn? After all, one of the strategies taken by American evangelicals after their theological and ecclesiastical defeat early in this century was to reduce involvement culturally and politically. Other than a brief period during the McCarthy years, when such groups as the Church League of America or The Christian Anti-Communist Crusade gained attention, the disaffected religious right remained relatively quiet. Indeed, for many, worldly involvement was specifically proscribed.

In tracking this feature of Conservative Protestantism's curious path we might note first of all that the enemy has shifted significantly: from church and seminary to court and public education, for example. Similarly, therefore, the battleground has switched from *ecclesiastical* politics to community, state, and national politics. Nothing reflects this change so well as noting Conservative Protestants' main target: "secular humanism." What agencies embody secular humanism? Not liberal churches surely: God is still their focus; the sacred is still present in their endeavors. It is, rather, agencies like courts, elementary and secondary schools, hospitals, colleges, the mass media, and the entertainment industry that, by leaving out God altogether, raise the ire of Conservative Protestants. It is the United Nations and, on occasion, the State Department. These are the agencies "captured" by secular humanism in the view of conservative Protestants.

The consequence has been a necessary shift of attention therefore. For example, in the Pro-Family Forum's pamphlet, "Is Humanism Molesting Your Child?"[15] the platform of the "religion of secular humanism" is identified. In only a few instances are its planks theological (e.g., "denies the Biblical account of creation"), most being instead political and cultural (e.g., "believes in sexual freedom" or "believes in control of the environment"). It seems reasonable to suppose that the more political and cultural the objection, the more political must the response become. It is one thing to give up the fight if one's enemies do not *believe* correctly, but it is another when they *behave* improperly. Political involvement is almost compelled under these circumstances.

With this shift in mind, then, we can take note of a second feature of the present-day scene: the *political* right has sought out and joined forces with the *religious* right at least as much as the reverse. To put it simply (though accurately, even by its own testimony) the Moral Majority would have existed with or without a Baptist clergyman at its helm, for it was not so much a theological as a moral organization.

The question remains, however, why conservative Protestants now would join in political battle when, in the past, they have been reluctant to do so. The conspiritorial answer is easy: they are being duped by the *political* right wing, an answer having some merit when one considers that Phyllis Schlafly and Richard Viguerie are Roman Catholic; Howard Phillips, Jewish; Paul Weyrich, Eastern Rite; and Orrin Hatch, Mormon. More benignly, one can assume that for some Protestant conservatives, some moral goals transcend their Protestant particularism.

Still, for many Protestant conservatives, political goals do *not* transcend religious particularism, meaning that nationally this religious constituency has been difficult to organize and meaning further that there is little likelihood the radical religious Right will capture either political party or make much of a dent if it begins its own. It also means that where Conservative Protestantism *has* been effective politically, it has been largely at the local level, on issues capable of generating a more homogeneous involvement; for example, over the question of library books. The Christian Right can be stirred politically, in other words, but it is by no means of one mind with the agenda of the political Right.[16]

This last observation thus raises the final issue to be discussed in this essay: What is the wider social meaning of conservative Protestantism's current status?

CONCLUSION

Recall the point made earlier that one factor helping to establish Evangelical Protestantism as a national creed in the nineteenth century was its sanctioning of "libertarianism and traditionalism." This combination was called *paradoxical* because, as Tocqueville, for one, saw so clearly, ancient regimes exalted traditionalism but therefore discouraged libertarianism, thus suggesting that if a democracy encouraged libertarianism, it would mean the end of tradition. That this did not happen in America puzzled Tocqueville; and he found the explanation primarily in evangelical religion, which encouraged what he called "self-interest rightly understood"; that is, libertarianism *tempered* by traditionalism. In effect, Americans favored both change and continuity; they worshipped both capitalism *and* God. And this combination worked for nearly a century. It worked because the economy expanded, and it worked because consensus was largely maintained on what tradition—God—meant.

But the forces of modernity broke the consensus. First to go was the theological consensus, initially by the inclusion of Catholics and Jews as first-class religious citizens (even yet not acknowledged in a few Protestant quarters) and second, within Protestantism, by the "battle over the Bible," leading to the split at the turn of the century discussed earlier. If these disturbances had remained theological only, probably the camp identified as Conservative Protestant after 1920 would have remained primarily nonpolitical. But as we saw, there followed, forty years later, a disintegration also of the traditional *moral* consensus. This breakdown, it was suggested, reached symbolic culmination in the counterculture, and today is perhaps most sharply etched in the abortion issue.

To appreciate the reality, but also the profundity, of this breakdown, contrast the bumpers of two cars: one with stickers saying the Benevolent and Protective Order of Elks, the National Rifle Association, and Buy American; the other with stickers saying Equal Rights Amendment, Greenpeace, and Get out of El Salvador. One point is obvious; an observer can infer from the bumper stickers quite a bit of the moral philosophy of the two drivers. But what of their religion? Their party? *If* both drivers are religious and Protestant, the first probably leans toward theological conservatism, the second toward modernism. And, as research has shown, the first is probably a Republican, the second a Democrat. If, however, both drivers are secular, driver A is just as likely to be Democrat, driver B Republican, though neither will feel comfortable with all of his or her party's platform.

But change the circumstances slightly. Let the Republican Party be led by a spokesperson for moral traditionalism, who talks like an economic libertarian. Suddenly evangelical Republicans find their historic creed being expressed, and Democratic traditionalists find warrant for switching their vote. Conservative Protestants thus seem to spring up all over the place, and the "popular" party becomes the Republican.

Something like this seems to have happened in America in the last decade and a half. Jimmy Carter held out some theological hope for Conservative Protestants in 1976 but quickly disqualified himself with his moral agenda: it was "modern." In 1980, therefore, Ronald Reagan drew off sizeable Democratic traditionalists on the basis of moral issues and managed to do so without losing many Republican modernists to the Democratic candidate. In 1984, this unbalanced switching seems simply to have intensified. George Bush, appearing fickle to many Americans, obviously has problems holding this coalition together.

Of course, political campaigns are vastly complicated things, and religious outlook is just one of the factors having an independent impact on persons' votes. In the 1980s, nevertheless, evangelicalism achieved a notoriety in the mass media it had not "enjoyed" since the 1920s, and this notoriety has been a result no doubt of its involvement in national politics. Its current resurgence thus cannot be understood as simply a theological phenomenon but must be understood as well as an event in America's cultural life. Such is the latest step on the curious path of Conservative Protestantism.

3

Cults and the Civil Relgion: A Tale of Two Centuries

INTRODUCTION

In the first two chapters we explored religion as it comes in the form of liberal and conservative Protestantism. American religion is larger than this, of course, as the United States, like all modern nations, has grown increasingly pluralistic. Perhaps most non-Protestant religions in America have come with immigrants, but some, often called *cults*, have resulted from foreign missionaries come to these shores. During the 1960s and 1970s, we witnessed an extraordinary increase in the number, variety, and visibility of such cults. Not the only significant social change during this time, of course, nor uniquely American, nevertheless the many—and unusual—religious movements of this period will be remembered as one of the distinctive marks of the period.

Many explanations for this spiritual explosion have been offered, one of which sees the new cults[1] as a response to the corruption and trivialization of the American civil religion. Advanced most forcefully by Robert Bellah,[2] this explanation presumes that Americans generally regard their nation in transcendental terms, conceive it as having a sacred (God-ordained) mission among nations and thus are profoundly disturbed when such a mission is violated. The cold war following World War II, the argument goes on, heated up illegitimately in Southeast Asia, brought to a halt the promise of advance in civil rights, and culminated in the shabby reign of Richard Nixon, so well symbolized by the scandal of Watergate. Thus, their civil religion having been corrupted, Americans were faced with an ideological void, which was then filled by one or another heterodox or exotic theology. So goes the theory.

Certain features of this argument are especially attractive. First, the postwar years saw no let-up in the use of civil religious symbols, even as the consensus of the 1940s eroded and reached a calamitous low during the Vietnam war. A cynicism about the American civil religion might well be expected under these circumstances, and indeed flag decals became the badge not of unity but of religiopolitical division; some posted it in car windows, others sewed it on trouser seats.

Second, as many have noted about the current wave of cults, many of them exhibit a strong antitechnological streak, thus suggesting a revolt against America as model of modernity. Whether challenging "straight" middle-class niceties, the "competitiveness" of the corporate world, or the exploitative approach to the environment, the new religious movements were more centrifugal than centripetal, more eccentric than central, more divergent than integrative of core American values.

Third, the largest source of recruits for the new movements were found not among the economically or socially deprived but among the middle classes, whose "alienation" must therefore be explained not in terms of money or prestige but otherwise.

Fourth, insofar as cultic activity was the response to the corruption of the American civil religion, the alien flavor of the cults, especially of the Eastern mystical kind, takes on special significance. As a former devotee of the Radha Soami Satsang of Beas (Los Angeles) wrote of his attraction to it: "To express our distrust, we needed a vocabulary that came from outside the world we doubted."

To sum up, the explanation states that the American civil religion was at a low ebb, and cults were an understandable result. If it became impossible still to believe that God blessed this nation and meant it to lead all other nations; if it seemed implausible that American institutions, being built upon divine law, were therefore self-correcting; if pride of nation and optimism about its future sounded hollow; then it became repugnant for many to "be" American—to derive their primary identity from citizenship in this nation-state. Instead, they immersed themselves in cults. If the Kingdom of God could no longer be sought in the land of the Pilgrim's pride, it would be sought in other traditions.

AMERICAN CIVIL RELIGION IN 1830s AND 1840s

This explanation is confounded, however, by another period in American history. The first decades of the nineteenth century, especially the 1830s and 1840s, seem to contradict the proposition that cults arise during a time of national pessimism or diminished faith in the civil religion. If the 1960s and 1970s mark an ebb tide in the American civil religion, surely the period from Stonewall Jackson's defeat of the British at New Orleans in 1815 until the passage of the Fugitive Slave Law in 1850 marks its flood tide. But in this earlier time, a time of optimism and growing national faith, we observe not only religious orthodoxy and tranquility but also, much like the 1960s and 1970s, a rich assortment of new religious movements and spiritual experimentation. In this earlier period also, people were attracted to cults. But God seemed to be blessing, not forsaking, the nation.

Consider first the signs of a robust civil religion. The war of independence had been won, and the resulting constitutional government was functioning well. The acquisition of vast lands soon followed: the Louisiana Purchase in 1803 and Florida in 1819 confirmed America's geographic destiny early in the century (as the addition of Texas, the Oregon Territory, and California was to do in the 1840s). Jackson's defeat of the British provided international military evidence for what was domestically believed about this divinely inspired national experiment: America's freedom and democracy make her superior to all other nations.

CULTIC ACTIVITY IN THE 1830s AND 1840s

Consider now the religious situation of the 1830s and 1840s. Given the "explanation" reviewed above for the rise of cults in the 1960s and 1970s we would have expected quiescence on the religious front in the early nineteenth century. Instead, we read accounts remarkably similar to the current scene. In 1840 the Friends of Universal Reform, an association of unorthodox groups, met in convention, prompting this description by Ralph Waldo Emerson:

A great variety of dialect and of costume was noticed; a great deal of confusion, eccentricity and freak appeared, as well as of zeal and enthusiasm. If the assembly was disorderly, it was picturesque. Madmen, madwomen, men with beards, Dunkers, Muggletonians, Come-Outers, Groaners, Agrarians, Seventh-day Baptists, Quakers, Abolitionists, Calvinists, Unitarians and Philosophers,—all came successively to the top, and seized their moment, if not their hour, wherein to chide, or pray, or preach, or protest.[3]

If the 1960s were the era of "tune in, turn on, drop out," the 1830s and 1840s evidenced a similar rejection of social participation. Emerson again describes, this time the young: "their solitary and fastidious manners not only withdraw them from the conversation, but from the labors of the world; they are not good citizens, not good members of society; unwillingly they bear their part of the public and private burdens; they do not share in the public charities, in the public religious rites."[4] Even the rallying cry of the 1960s, to "do your own thing," has its origin in Emerson's famous essay "Self-Reliance." Having told his readers they must reject social convention and follow their own path, Emerson concluded with the exhortation "But do your thing, and I shall know you." Many were the opportunities provided by the cults of the national period for people to do just that.

Think of the horror the parents of the day must have felt when their children became members of a nineteenth-century group called the *Pilgrims*. Under the dictatorship of a fellow named Bullard, the Pilgrims practiced economic communism and placed a ban on washing, shaving, and bathing. William Miller's cult of the second Advent was equally bizarre. Based on elaborate mathematical calculations, Miller determined 1843 as the year in which Christ would return to earth in triumph. Miller's prophecy convinced many thousands of people.

Has the present age been characterized by an upsurge of interest in the occult? People of the national period were also fascinated by mesmerism, clairvoyance, phrenology, and astrology. Andrew Jackson Davis, the "Poughkeepsie Seer," wrote the Urantia Book of his day, a hodgepodge of spiritualist doctrine composed in a trance and entitled *The Harmonial Philosophy*. This volume went through thirty-four editions in less than thirty years. Spiritualist circles became common in hundreds of Northeastern towns.

If contemporary observers find it hard to believe that anyone could take seriously a man like Jim Jones or the Rev. Moon, what would have been their opinion of the formation of the Mormon Church? Joseph Smith claimed to have found a pile of golden tablets inscribed with an unknown language. With the aid of the magic spectacles, Urim and Thummin, Smith read and dictated a translation of those tablets. Though the tablets disappeared, their revelations became the basis of Mormonism. One can imagine the reaction with which friends and parents greeted the news that a loved one had converted to this outlandish new cult.

Would parents have been any happier to find that their progeny had become Shakers? Mother Anne Lee, the founder of the Shaker cult, believed that God was both masculine and feminine, Christ's mission having been the incarnation of the masculine side of the deity and Mother Anne now the incarnation of the feminine side. Mother Anne's belief was that sexual lust was the root source of all human evil; the Shakers were strict celibates.

John Humphrey Noyes's Oneida community offered another cultic option. Believing that Jesus had already returned to earth during the second generation of Christians, Noyes held that the new age had begun, that people must now live a life fully in the spirit. They could be perfect if they realized it. Noyes's community abolished private property and private relationships because of their belief that perfect persons would be completely unselfish. These assumptions led to the institution of "complex marriage" in which Noyes distinguished "amative" from procreative functions of sexual intercourse. Under the terms of complex marriage, amative sexual contacts in as many ways as possible were encouraged. The sexual sensibility of the nineteenth-century must have regarded such free love cultish indeed.

Other utopian communes abounded. Adin Ballou sought, through his Hopedale community, to inaugurate the kingdom of heaven on earth. The Fruitlands commune of Bronson Alcott and Charles Lane eschewed the use of cotton (because produced by slave labor) and the use of all animals for food, clothing, or labor. Brook Farm, the communal living experiment of the Transcendentalists, hoped to achieve a noble existence through a combination of honest manual labor and the life of the intellect. The belief in the improvement of the individual through simple communal living, so characteristic of many in the 1960s and 1970s, can be observed just as readily during the early middle years of the nineteenth century.

Moreover, we find not just the cultic appeal of communitarianism and individualism in the 1830s and 1840s, but also parallels to such other modern signs as long hair on men and revulsion toward etiquette. We find an attraction to the unspoiled outdoors—even to a population still largely rural! And we find the fascination with the Oriental, the mystical, and, in some instances, the authoritarian.

All of this, however, occurred in a period of unsurpassed civil religious fervor. If we would retain our first thesis—that cults emerge in response to a corrupted civil religion, to civil religion at its nadir—then it appears we must accept also the antithesis: cults emerge in response to a particularly vibrant civil religion, to civil religion at the high point.

IN SEARCH OF RESOLUTION

How might this apparent contradiction be resolved? If cultic activity and the civil religion are related in America, how might we explain the appearance of many cults not only during a period of corrupt national faith but also during a period when it is robust? What, in other words, is *common* to both high and low periods in the American civil religion?

One answer is clear: *self-consciousness as an American citizen.* The identity that, during "normal" times is made salient only during patriotic rituals and then in a low key, is, during periods of national boom or bust, an identity with far more intrusive power. Instead of an American self—superficially activated only by July Fourth oratory, a Presidential inauguration, or the Olympic Games, citizens during either boom or bust times have their Americanness constantly before them. Headlines scream it out, and daily conversations lock it in. It becomes nearly impossible to "forget" that one is, at core, an American.

This core identity of Americans, however, as so many analysts (foreign as well as domestic) have noted, contains a "religious" element; it is not merely political. That is to say, although high and low points in the fortunes of other nations also activate the civic consciousness of their citizens, few nations have, as G. K. Chesterton put it, "the soul of a church."[5] In Americans then, when citizenship is activated, so also is religion. For example, during ordinary times a newly built public school might be named with little or no fanfare. Should the name Washington or Franklin or Lincoln be chosen, or even George Washington Carver or Albert Einstein or Public School 118, there is little public concern. But during either a time of national pride and optimism or a time of national shame and pessimism, such name selection becomes a public issue. Why? Because what is at stake is the control of collective symbols, and these collective symbols in the case of America are more than merely political; they are religious as well, meaning that the profoundest convictions of Americans are involved.

Understanding this peculiarity of American culture, that is, having a clear grasp of how and when the American civil religion is expressed, allows us to resolve the apparent paradox in this tale of two centuries. For in both periods, a number of American citizens had reason to question their nation's behavior and thus their own role as citizens. In the 1830s and 1840s the new nation was beginning to experience the forces of industrialization, urbanization, and immigration. As a result, although many persons rode the wave of optimism, others experienced dislocation and therefore doubt over national policy. Moreover, the national experiment was enough advanced to cause some persons, motivated by the very nobility of that experiment, to point to the gap between ideal and actuality. Altogether, as Mathews put it: "The revolution had created great anticipation for the future; but the kind of future people wanted was not easily realized. The result was a vague uneasiness that created a general susceptibility to social movements."[6]

To be sure, doubt about one's role as an American did not take the same form in the 1960s and 1970s. But certainly held up for scrutiny were the rights and responsibilities accompanying American citizenship. And once again, a significant base of the questioning for many, was the gap between national behavior and noble ideal. In both time periods, in other words, the profoundest meaning of America—its very location in the transcendent order—was called to account by a significant portion of the population.

TRACKING DOWN THE INDEPENDENT VARIABLE

In questioning the legitimacy of their government, citizens in both the nineteenth and twentieth centuries were thus likely to invoke the civil religion, even though in the earlier time national optimism prevailed and in the later time pessimism. Their quarrel, after all, was not simply political; no mere change in regimes would satisfy them. Nor was their quarrel narrowly religious; they were not church rebels upset with the theological establishment's failure to meet their spiritual needs.[7] The people of whom we speak, therefore, can be called *civil religious* rebels. They were disturbed by their nation's deviation from a path they saw as transcendent in meaning. Their objection, to put it differently, was sacredly principled—religious if not ecclesiastical.

The situation in recent years appears to fit this explanation well. Much dissent over civil rights and the Vietnam War has been purely political, but another significant response has been cultic, attraction to an alien religious ideology. But, one can ask, why a *religious* response, and an alien one at that, if the disillusionment is *civil*? The answer, of course, lies in the unique blurring of patriotism and piety to be found in America. It is not that all civil dissent must take religious form, but rather religion is a likely alternative if it is one's patriotism that is called into question.

Especially will this be the case among those who are not "failures" under prevailing sociopolitical arrangements. Failures (and their sympathizers) under the status quo, if not narrowly political in their protest, are likely to be attracted to sects; that is, find fault with established churches and seek for their condition in this life a justification in the next life. This is, of course, the classic Marxian formulation.

Such persons no doubt can be found (during both periods under review), but they have not provided the recruits for *cults* (i.e., alien ideologies) in the 1960s and 1970s. Rather, cultic recruits have been precisely those who, having no *personal* complaint with either the political or religious arrangements, nonetheless reject *in principle* the course their nation has followed. These cultic recruits, to put it differently, have been overwhelmingly from the middle-class, establishment mainstream, not the exploited, marginal lower class.

But if the model seems to fit well the twentieth century, what of the nineteenth? Were those cult members also civil religious, not merely political or merely religious, rebels? When we look beneath the optimistic rhetoric of the period 1825-1860, we certainly observe a nation in the midst of radical change. Elkins says this was a period in which "limits were being broken everywhere, in which traditional expectations were disrupted profoundly—a classic instance of that tension-producing state which Emile Durkheim named 'anomie.' It was against such a background that Transcendentalism and other reform movements first appeared."[8]

We discover, in other words, that at the heart of social criticism registered by the sensitive souls of the nineteenth century was profound disgust with America's rampant materialism and unethical economic competition. Emerson, the most penetrating social observer of his day, reflected: "It cannot be wondered that this general inquest into abuses should arise in the bosom of society, when one considers the practical impediments that stand in the way of virtuous young men. The young man, on entering life, finds the way to lucrative employments blocked with abuses. The ways of trade are grown selfish to the borders of theft, and supple to the borders (if not beyond the borders) of fraud."⁹ The result is that,

> many intelligent and religious persons withdraw themselves from the common labors and competitions of the market and the caucus, and betake themselves to a certain solitary and critical way of living, from which no solid fruit has yet appeared to justify their separation. They hold themselves aloof; they feel the disproportion between their faculties and the work offered them, and they prefer to ramble in the country and perish of ennui, to the degradation of charities and such ambitions as the city can propose to them. They are striking work, and crying out for somewhat worthy to do!¹⁰

Emerson's is a perfect description of a sacred but centrifugal response to social dissatisfaction: the young found "somewhat worthy to do" in cultic activity.

Social criticism in the nineteenth century was not confined to economics. As the slavery question heated up, and as the Southern hold on the executive branch made possible the violation of civil rights (e.g., interdiction of the mail and suppression of free speech), many became critical of the government in general and turned to cultic activity. Many abolitionists, for example, unable to impress their reforms on their churches and their government, "promptly repudiated American institutions and plunged into the work of organizing perfect communities of their own."¹¹

Government action such as the removal of the Cherokee Indians (1837), the Mexican War (1846), and the Fugitive Slave Law (1850) also engendered a great deal of civil rebelliousness that erupted in cultic activity. Thoreau, himself a one-man cult, was jailed for protesting government malfeasance by refusing to pay taxes. In his *Anti-Slavery and Reform Papers*, Thoreau justifies his civil disobedience: "when a sixth of the population of a nation which has undertaken to be the refuge of liberty are slaves, and a whole country [Mexico] is unjustly overrun and conquered by a foreign army, and subjected to military law, I think that it is not too soon for honest men to rebel and revolutionize."¹² Hence arose the "solitary nullifiers" so ably described by Emerson:

In politics, for example, it is easy to see the progress of dissent. The country is full of rebellion; the country is full of kings. Hands off: let there be not control and no interference in the administration of the affairs of this kingdom of me. . . . So the country is frequently affording solitary examples of resistance to the government, solitary nullifiers, who throw themselves on their reserved rights; nay, who have reserved all their rights; who reply to the assessor and to the clerk of court that they do not know the State, and embarrass the courts of law by non-juring and the commander-in-chief of the militia by non-resistance.[13]

These "solitary nullifiers" in the political realm were the very persons most likely to participate in proliferating cults of their day.

CONCLUSION

That these civil rebels—from pessimism and revulsion in the twentieth century, from criticism of misguided optimism in the nineteenth— express their rebellion religiously is precisely the point, of course. Scratch an American in his or her identity and not just political but religious blood will likely flow. A nation with the soul of a church will, when soulfully wounded, likely count religion among its responses.

Therefore, and here of course is the religiopolitical uniqueness of America, civil rebelliousness is seldom merely political but rather is civil religious. When it occurs, it can be expressed adequately neither through "pure" politics nor through established religion. The very features of American history and culture that make "being" American a religious phenomenon also make it likely that civil protest will be registered with alien religious symbols. For the same reason that the politically unusual is religiously freighted ("godless communism"), so is civil dissent likely to require for its expression a religious rhetoric drawn from outside the American ecclesiastical mainstream. As W. Clark Roof puts it: "Mainline religious institutions are identified with the established order, closely akin to the dominant values of society, and thus rejection of one often entails abandonment of the other."[14]

We are, it might be said, turning on its head the famed thesis of Will Herberg.[5] If being a Protestant, a Catholic, or a Jew are but alternative religious ways to *be* an American—to express the American civil religion, if you please—then doubt about that civil religion requires expression drawn from outside Protestantism, Catholicism, or Judaism. Cultic activity, in this view, is thus not simply a *revulsion against* the religious establishment any more than *participation in* that establishment is simply a sign of commitment to the particularistic claims of one's denomination. Cultic activity, by this account, is rather a declaration of dissent from the path one's society is taking. This link between civil religion and the cults is the same, then, whether the dissent occurs in the midst of national folly and despair (the case in the 1960s and 1970s) or of national expansion and enthusiasm (the case a century and a half earlier).

American civil religion, as we have conceived of it here, is thus evanescent indeed. During most of American history it has not even been clearly differentiated from other social values. Instead, it has existed, in John F. Wilson's words, "as a dimension or aspect of the society which is present 'in, with, and under' the whole."[16] During the periods on which we have been focusing, it happens that the civil religion was a prominent feature of national awareness, but this sometimes-only prominence should not call into question its reality. The American civil religion is no less real because its creed is only periodically invoked and never formalized, its organization made up of volunteers who may not even be aware of their membership, its rituals generally practiced under nonreligious auspices, its saints so infused into folklore as to mask their sacred quality, and its prophets so often despised in their own lifetimes that tragedy stalks them. There is, one might say, no "church" of the American civil religion, and thus it is hard to see, hear, and touch. But it is nonetheless real.

When crises come, and when individuals define such occasions to be not of their making but the nation's, then what it means to be American comes to the fore. Perhaps generally the question is clear, the answer nearly unanimous. American response to World War II is a case in point. In some instances, however, the situation is exceedingly difficult, either because of genuine confusion over the question or because of severe disagreement over the answer. In the first part of the nineteenth century, we suggest, anxiety occurred over the question; What did it mean to "be" an American? What were the limits of economic competition, of nationalism, and above all, of slavery in terms of the American creed? By the late 1960s, in contrast, division occurred over the answer: was America the beacon for all nations or their invader? the home of the free or of ineradicable racial barriers? the land of bounty or of multinational corporate booty?

Clear questions and unanimous answers will mean religious business as usual. Dissatisfaction will then be felt by individuals qua individuals, and they may protest within their religious traditions for sectarian solutions to their misfortunes. They may, alternatively, protest within their political traditions.

But the issue may get muddy, and the responsibility may shift from individual to nation. What *is* America supposed to be and do? And thus what is a person *as an American* supposed to be and do? Such an issue, we are arguing, evokes in America what can rightfully be called the civil religion. When evoked, the civil religion in turn calls forth a number of different responses, attraction to cults being only one, of course. But American history suggests that the cultic response is not uncommon; the religious events of the last twenty-five years, as bizarre as some have been, are in a tradition as old as the nation itself.

Part Two

Evangelicalism and Politics

4

An Approach to the Political Meaning of Evangelicalism in Present-Day America

INTRODUCTION

The centrality of religion in society, as the Preface suggested, may fluctuate in a manner that religion's sovereignty cannot. The unexpected (?) increased popularity of Evangelical Protestantism in recent decades offers the occasion to examine this notion in some detail.

Few people will deny that America, once again, is experiencing a religious revival. To be sure, some skepticism is called for whenever large-scale change in the American religious scene is declared because, relative to most nations, Americans have always been very religious. A cynic can point out, as S. M. Lipset did about the revival of the 1950s, and Garry Wills did about the present,[1] that what is new is not so much the behavior as the attention to the behavior; Americans, the cynic will say, have always been church goers, donors to religious causes, prayerful at home, Bible readers, or whatever.

One response to such skepticism, however, is to point out that renewed attention to religion is itself a religious phenomenon worthy of understanding. Perhaps it is also safe in the present instance to assume that behind the visible signs noted in the mass media lie some changes as well in the *meaning* of people's behavior. After all, posting a bumper sticker on one's automobile declaring "Jesus Is Lord" is an act embedded in motive and effect, whether the sentiment being expressed is long standing or new. And what can be stated is that more Americans have been posting bumper stickers on their autos. They are also watching televised religious programs in unprecedented number, marching in antiabortion or pro-prayer demonstrations, and trying to get creationism into the public school curriculum. Something new in the American religious sphere *is* going on.

My concern here will be confined to that segment of the religious scene called *evangelicalism*, a movement within Protestant Christianity, often identified with Arminianism, that conceives of salvation as the personal act of "accepting" Jesus as savior and puts a premium on sharing this viewpoint (hence the acceptance, by both insider and observer, of the label *evangelical* to describe this theological position). Often associated with fundamentalism, evangelicalism indeed includes a great many who are antimodern in biblical scholarship, antiurban in lifestyle, and anticommunist in political preference. Rut evangelicalism in present day America also includes many who are distinctly "modernist," urban, or left wing, who subscribe without fundamentalist flavor to the creed of Jesus as personal savior.

Stripped of its Protestant qualities, this evangelicalism is found elsewhere in American life, of course. It shares in the general accent on "feeling" sweeping across the nation, taking the form of antibureaucracy, grow your own food, home delivery of babies, sentimentalism about the wilderness, and so forth. In the life of religious organizations, it is found in Judaism in the *chavurah* movement, in Catholicism in the charismatic movement, and, throughout church life, in such popular activities as marriage encounter, family retreats, lay participation in worship, and so on. Evangelicalism, then, is but one part of a larger whole.

A question arises, however, about the nature of that whole. What is the substance of the larger phenomenon of which evangelicalism is part? Generally speaking, two answers have been offered. For some, the evangelical movement is but the religious expression of the narcissistic "me decade." It shares a whole, in other words, that includes the encounter-group movement, sexual revisionism, high divorce rates, low voter turnout, and the therapeutic ethic generally. Having given up on the impersonal society as a source of meaning and reward, people are increasingly turning inward, and one way to turn inward—a religious way—is to become evangelical. At least Jesus loves me![2]

Another model of the whole is quite different, however. Without denying that American society contains the centrifugal forces just described, forces atomizing the population, this alternative model sees in evangelicalism not the *expression* of self-concern but its antidote. The whole of which evangelicalism is a part according to *this* view, then, includes the environmental protection movement, consumer organizations, political parties, and protest groups. Rather than being the religious channel by which people are *atomized*, evangelicalism is the religious channel by which they *participate* in society. The 1980 U.S. Presidential campaign, wherein the Moral Majority or Christian Roundtable became so evident, in this view, was not an egocentric aberration but rather the latest manifestation of a recurring phenomenon in American history: religion's impact on the political life of this nation.[3]

The issue, then, is whether current evangelicalism is but one more cocoon, another haven from the onslaught of modern life, or whether it is a critical force drawing individuals back into society. If the first, then evangelicalism in America today has no particular political meaning other than perhaps the narcotizing effect of drawing evangelicals away from the political arena. If the second however, historians in the next century will look upon the last third of the twentieth century as another turning point in the religiopolitical development of American society.

THE LESSON OF TOCQUEVILLE

Alexis de Tocqueville came to America in 1831 ostensibly to study prisons but even more because he was fascinated by the American experiment in democracy, about which he wrote his justly famous analysis. His understanding of democracy (or equality, what we would now call the decline of ascriptive status) led him to the gloomy prediction that despotism was its natural outcome:

> Individualism is of democratic origin and threatens to grow as conditions get more equal. . . . Among democratic peoples, new families continually rise from nothing while others fall, and nobody's position is quite stable. . . . All a man's interests are

limited to those near himself. . . . They form the habit of thinking of themselves in isolation and imagine that their whole destiny is in their own hands. . . . Despotism, by its very nature sus-
picious, sees the isolation of men as the best guarantee of its
own permanence.[4]

TWO CHANNELS

However, finding not despotism in America but what he called "republican democracy," Tocqueville was led to search out the factors contra-
vening despotism. He found several, including geography, a bill of
rights, and multiple layers of government. But whatever the factor, its
countervailing impact on despotism was directed through one of two
channels.[5] One of these channels is any institutional arrangement bringing people together, thus overcoming "isolation" and providing a conduit for collective political interests. The other channel is the perspective
of natural law, belief in the existence of laws lying beyond human nego-
tiation or choice, that thus represents shared values in the presence of
obvious heterogeneity. The first of these channels gave rise to Tocqueville's emphasis on the voluntary association; Americans formed
themselves into organizations to accomplish almost every task, he said,
and were thereby prevented from atomizing, as despotism would have
them do. The second channel led to Tocqueville's emphasis on "self-
interest rightly understood," the public spiritedness by which one's
selfish concerns are constrained in the belief that a higher, common
good exists.

Anybody reading Tocqueville's analysis of these channels for
countervailing forces to despotism cannot help but be struck with the
unusual attention he gives to churches and religion. Indeed, much of
Democracy in America is about religious beliefs, behavior, organization,
and leadership. Churches were the single most important voluntary
association he observed, responsible as they were for the taming of the
frontier by bringing people together not only for worship but for building schools, hospitals, and colleges, creating missionary societies, cir-
culating news, and much else as well.

Moreover, churches, via sermon and Sunday School lesson, promulgated a common theology—a civil religion, we might say today—
wherein denominational differences were muted, and self-interests
could therefore be "rightly understood." In America, Tocqueville wrote,

people "zealously perform all the external duties of religion" (p. 259), but though "American Christians are divided into very many sects, they all see their religion in the same light" (p. 449).

The result? "The longer I stayed in the country, the more conscious I became of the important political consequences resulting from this novel religious situation" (p. 295). It is clear that, for Tocqueville, the church and religion constitute fundamental building blocks in the maintenance of society. What is equally clear, however, is the fact that, had Tocqueville visited thirty years earlier or thirty years later, his observations on the political consequences of religion might have been markedly different. Why?

AWAKENINGS IN AMERICA

On several occasions in America's history, waves of religious fervor have swept over the country, leaving in their wake consequences neither intended nor immediately recognized.[6] The three decades just prior to Tocqueville's visit constituted one of these occasions, a movement generally known as the *Second Great Awakening*. Its causes were many, and its expression took somewhat varying form in New England, the South, and the Western frontier. But everywhere it channeled religiousness into action. It was the consequences of the Second Great Awakening, then, that the perceptive Frenchman observed as he toured New England, the South, and the frontier territory in the 1830s, remarking on the central role played by religion in American democracy.

Church historians note that during this period, for example, the Methodist and Baptist denominations grew to commanding size through their willingness to send earnest, if crude, preachers into even the smallest of settlements; Tocqueville observed the central role played by preacher and church in "organizing" communities via voluntary associations. Church historians, as another example, point to the Awakening as the source of the moral reform mentality so characteristic of mid-nineteenth-century America; Tocqueville observed that churches encouraged "right understanding" of downplaying denominational particularism and accenting the common moral code. The two channels of countervailing forces to despotism—social participation and common values—were thus channels brought into existence and made effective in significant part by the wave of emotional religiousness preceding Tocqueville's visit.[7]

THE SITUATION TODAY

The issue identified in the opening pages of this essay is now clearly seen: Is the evangelicalism of present-day America another in the series of awakenings? And if it is, will its political consequences resemble those of 1800-1830, an enhanced social participation and a more common value outlook? Or will it contribute to further particularism, atomization and—as Tocqueville feared—despotism?

The answer cannot confidently be given at this time, inasmuch as we are in the midst even yet of identifying and charting the phenomenon itself; its effects must be measured sometime in the future. Nonetheless a scheme of analysis can be offered, a scheme borrowed from Tocqueville and refined by contemporary sociological theory. With this scheme we at least have categories of analysis and thus locations in which to place the otherwise stray data as they become available. This scheme can be diagrammed as follows:

	Channel of Influence	
Level of Influence	Social Participation	Common Values
Individual	?	?
Structural	?	?
Cultural	?	?

To put the matter another way, we can look for evidence at each of three levels bearing on the question whether either or both of two channels, social participation and common values, are facilitated or inhibited by evangelicalism.

INDIVIDUAL INFLUENCES

Data so far available probably bear most directly on the individual level of influence because they result from public opinion surveys. Thus, good evidence exists for the assertion that about 20 percent of American adults identify themselves as evangelical Christians.[8] For a modern, so-called secular nation, that percentage is, of course, surprisingly large, because it means that one in five report having had a "born-again" experience and report accepting a literal interpretation of the Bible. On the other hand, what is at issue here is not "how many?" but "with what effect?" What does the record show?

The Gallup organization conducted two surveys a decade ago in which a random sample of adult Americans were asked a number of religious questions. One survey was commissioned by the evangelical magazine, *Christianity Today*, to determine the size of the evangelical population and some of its characteristics.⁹ The other was commissioned by the National Council of Churches, especially to learn more about those persons unattached to any church.¹⁰ Both surveys contain items for sorting out evangelicals from others. We learn, therefore, that evangelicals, far from being atomized or isolated, are much more involved in church than are nonevangelicals. Moreover, their involvement takes the form not only of attendance at worship service but also of engaging in voluntary work through the church. Something of Tocqueville's voluntary association spirit does seem to be evident.

On the other hand, there is evidence of evangelicals' worldly withdrawal. Although they are more inclined, by nearly a two-to-one margin over nonevangelicals, to believe churches should speak out on political and economic matters, their priorities as Christians reduce *actual* political and community involvement to relatively minor importance. A quarter of Liberal Protestants and Roman Catholics (and one-half of the unaffiliated) regard such actual involvement as fundamentally important to the religious life; only 9 percent of evangelicals do.¹¹

Through the common values channel the evidence also appears mixed. A survey from early in 1980, underwritten by an insurance company to explore American values and beliefs, found what the study's director called "a spiritual renaissance" built on an earlier morality, severely challenged by the events of the 1960s and 1970s but now making a comeback. In a similar vein, Gallup has found a reversal in the long-term decline in the percent of Americans saying religion is very important in their lives. By no means returned to the 1952 level, this percentage has nonetheless undergone a significant increase in recent years; among Protestants and Catholics, men and women, young and old.¹²

And yet signals also appear that individual evangelicals regard their religious position as a warrant for denying other persons their religious positions. Most noteworthy, perhaps, was the declaration by one evangelical church leader that God does not hear the prayers of Jews inasmuch as they are not directed through Jesus. One might make the same interpretation (though less dramatically) of individual evangelicals who would return to state-sponsored prayers in public schools, restrict the civil rights of homosexuals on biblical grounds, impose the creation story as contained in the Bible onto the biology curriculum of public schools, and so forth. In other words, for all the evidence that individuals are undergoing a meaningful change of spirit, additional evidence suggests that the change is not necessarily public spirited, aimed to include and incorporate; it may instead be exclusionary and alienating.

STRUCTURAL INFLUENCES

Evidence at the structural level is less secure because it involves even more selection than does evidence on the individual level. We know that the Moral Majority (a right-wing political adjunct of the evangelical movement, now defunct) at one point claimed a half-million members, and the Christian Voice (also an organization devoted to election campaigning and legislative influence) claimed nearly half that membership size. There exists also a "left-wing" evangelical movement, which has its own journals and network of influence, though less money apparently.[13] Possibly the summary meaning of such stray facts is found in Gallup's observation that, although evangelicals tend to be drawn from those segments of the population less inclined to vote, evangelicals in fact participate at a rate commensurate with nonevangelicals.[14] Thus, one structural impact of evangelicalism is to enhance the participation of evangelicals in the political process.

The *direction* of any such participation is not so clear, however. Tocqueville noted that Americans in the nineteenth century pursued their self-interests in such a fashion that the collective welfare was also served. The question arises now toward the end of the twentieth century whether the religious motivation for political and community involvement is likewise public spirited, or whether it is instead the single-minded fanaticism of persons hell bent on imposing their view of Christianity onto others.

Most mass media treatments of the Moral Majority and related organizations suggested that the latter portrait was more accurate. Those evangelicals who started so-called Christian schools as alternatives to tax-supported public schools, for example, are often identified as persons whose real motives are to avoid racially integrated education. The issue of school prayers or of abortion, as other examples, are offered in legislation designed to remove these issues from judicial review if they are passed, thus violating in spirit and in fact the historic balance-of-powers doctrine. As organizations, then, such evangelical political agencies are viewed with alarm by many for being antidemocratic, antiuniversalistic, and thus contrary to the spirit of common values.

Once again, however, the evidence clouds the scene. Lipset and Raab could find no data to support the Moral Majority's claim to have helped defeat certain liberal congressional candidates in the 1980 election,[15] and a comparable record of religious right-wing electoral failure has followed. A general shift toward political conservatism among American voters since 1980 is undeniable, of course, and certain liberal candidates have lost their seats. But in their careful search for evidence that organized, conservative, evangelical groups *added* anything to the general shift to the right, Lipset and Raab could find nothing in 1980, and similar analyses since have concluded likewise. Some of the reason for this seeming anachronism is found in Gallup's early 1980s data that the disapproval rate of the Moral Majority increased with increased information about it. Indeed, to find population sectors where approval of the Moral Majority equaled disapproval, one must arrive at the very sectors that—for reasons of low education, low income, and lack of sophistication—were really quite impotent politically.[16]

Moreover, one cannot equate all of the evangelical movement with right-wing politics. Although the evidence on this score is still incomplete, some data for example suggest that Carter benefitted more than Reagan from the evangelical vote of 1980. At the structural level, too, therefore, the channels of participation and common values appear to contain contradictory lessons.

CULTURAL INFLUENCES

At the cultural level, the situation again is ambiguous. Media attention alone implies something of evangelicalism's influence on popular culture. Christian rock music has entered popular entertainment via born-again musicians (even as others sharing their theology are still fighting show business as the modern Babylon). Fully half of all American adults, at least once a year during the 1980s, watched a televised religious program, a phenomenon known as the "electronic church," which once solicited millions of dollars each week, though now it is retrenching.[17] The publishing industry is not immune, as titles by the hundreds are published and bought by a public anxious to read yet one more tale of personal salvation from some prior degraded (but typically exciting) life of sin.[18] These books remain largely invisible to intellectuals, of course, because they do not attract scholarly review or other analysis by academic theologians. They nonetheless take their place as cultural signs of evangelical influence, as do Christian radio stations, Bible-study groups in college dormitories, evangelical athletic teams, and locker-room prayers. Indeed, since the mid-1970s there has been a steady increase in popular attention given to evangelicalism, according to a count of titles indexed in the *Reader's Guide to Periodical Literature*.

In terms of social participation, then, one might hazard the guess that, at the cultural level, evangelicals are encouraged to "come out of the closet." Here is part of the meaning of the automobile bumper stickers referred to earlier; some people's Christianity is being expressed more openly than in the past. From Presidential prayer breakfasts to public declarations by television stars, such cultural symbols probably encourage greater social involvement by evangelicals. Church going, to name simply one activity, becomes once again a culturally approved thing to do, and indeed the data show a leveling out in recent years of the long-term decline in church attendance and membership.[19] On this basis we might conclude, therefore, that, at the cultural level, participation is probably enhanced by evangelicalism.

Moreover, many evangelicals are rather fiercely "non" denominational; much of what they profess is avowedly not linked to membership in any particular organization. In this respect they resemble persons in the Second Great Awakening who likewise eschewed fancy labels and the status implications of belonging to one rather than another church body. Historic Protestant suspicions of liturgy, learned clergy, and formal requirements for membership, replaced by individual conviction and voluntary profession of faith, are seen once again in the current evangelical movement. *Within* evangelical circles, then, the expression of and commitment to common values is readily observed. Persons easily cross denominational lines to pursue collective ends, and on this basis we might conclude that, on the cultural level, so are common values enhanced.

On the other hand, if evangelicals easily cross denominational lines, they do not easily cross "faith" lines. Reference has been made already to the recent anti-Semitic eruption by an evangelical leader. The effect of such blatantly "political" eruptions is to expose, perhaps even create, factionalism among evangelicals. Thus, in the case of anti-Semitism, some in the evangelical camp regard Jews not as sinners for failing to accept Jesus as savior but as members of God's own Israel, necessary to fulfill the Second Coming. They are strong supporters of militarizing the state of Israel, a position not shared by others who in many respects share their theology. To cite another example, Billy Graham, who is something of a grandfather, if not midwife as well, to the current evangelical movement in America, publicly disavowed Jerry Falwell and the Moral Majority for being so political.

Certainly theological arguments for returning prayers to public schools are not designed to extend people's rights but to restrict them. The same might be said of theological arguments against equal rights for women, homosexuals, single parents, and possibly elective abortion. Rather than seek solutions satisfactory to everybody by anchoring them in values common to everybody, these evangelical positions seem designed instead to separate and engender hostility. Of course the attitudes of "evangelicals" are not all of one piece, as an earlier section of this chapter makes clear. The *legislative* effect of these attitudes is thus greatly attenuated once they enter the political arena. But the *cultural* effect is probably more divisive than homogenizing.

CONCLUSION

At all three levels then—individual, structural, and cultural—the evidence is decidedly mixed regarding the political meaning of America's current evangelical scene. Needless to say, evangelicalism is not uniquely American, so no scheme for determining its meaning can be drawn entirely from the history of the one society. Nonetheless, evangelical waves have washed across the American people on previous occasions, and when they did, political consequences of considerable magnitude followed. The question can appropriately be asked at this time, therefore, whether the current wave will resemble politically the others, and if so, how will the similarity come about.

It is here that Tocqueville's model is helpful. Granted, the answer is not yet apparent, but his analysis of the effects of the Second Great Awakening in the 1830s sensitizes us to the kind of evidence to which we should be alert in the waning years of the twentieth century. Summarizing that model into the notions of "social participation" and "common values," this essay has presented some illustrative data. Is evangelicalism more centripetal or centrifugal, for example? Does it enable its holders to join with believers of other creeds in the pursuit of shared

goals? And how about evangelicalism's effect? Does it encourage coop-
erative pursuit by suggesting the righteousness of mutuality, or is such
cooperation seen as simply necessary in an evil world, to be disdained if
self-interest is no longer served?

Depending on the answers to questions such as these, the evangelical movement may contribute to democratic society, the situation
Tocqueville diagnosed in 1831. On the other hand, the increased centrality indicated by a wave of religious fervor might contribute to the
tyranny Tocqueville feared. In the one instance, religious fervor could
lead to cooperation and commonality; in the other, to division and
therefore pursuit of selfishness. We must remember, however, that since
the 1830s Protestantism has declined in sovereignty. The consequences
of increased (or decreased) centrality are therefore muted, at least in
the political sphere. The political meaning of resurgent evangelicalism
in present-day America is consequently likewise muted. At least that is
the lesson to be learned from Tocqueville's model, rightly understood.

5

Political Evangelicalism: The Anglo-American Comparison

The question I address is why conservative Protestantism in the United States has taken such a political turn in recent years and, why, with a few exceptions, its British counterpart has not. I am mindful of two objections that surface immediately. The first is this: Has American evangelicalism *really* politicized, or is all the huffing and puffing really created by the mass media? Granted, the Moral Majority was real and Jerry Falwell is still real, but what actually happened? Such skepticism is good because it alerts us to a parallel issue we encounter later on, which has to do with the political *effectiveness* of Conservative Protestantism in the United States. So far, the effectiveness does not appear to be great, but nonetheless it can be argued that Evangelical Christians in America seem recently to have found reasons for engaging in political activities that only a few years ago had no appeal to them at all. Antiabortion efforts lead the way here, but so also have such issues as creationism, homosexuality, feminism, and pornography drawn evangelicals into the public arena, as did the two presidential campaigns of the 1980s, of course. On balance, then, I think it correct to say that Conservative Protestantism *has* politicized in recent years.

The second objection is almost the reverse of the first. "Has not evangelical Christianity always been political?" this objection asks. If consequences alone are considered, then probably the answer must be yes. From Martin Luther to John Calvin, from the Puritans in England and New England to the Methodists in coal mines and on the frontier, from those who would abolish slavery to those who would "evangelize the world in one generation," the political impact of antinomian religion has readily been apparent. But consequences alone are not what I refer to here. Certainly there is in Protestantism that theme Weber called "inner-worldly ascetism," and so also is there always, therefore, the potential for conceiving a new heaven and new earth with attendant political efforts to achieve them. But evangelicalism in the twentieth century, in both Britain and the United States, has been more a refuge for those unhappy with the direction the world is going than it has been the vehicle by which the world's direction is to be changed. And this "refuge" mentality gave Conservative Protestantism its apolitical character: one was evangelical *instead* of being politically engaged. At least that has been the pattern through most of the twentieth century. Now, late in this century the apolitical character has changed in America, though not to the same degree in Great Britain; and we are asking why by comparing the situations in the two societies.

SOME PRIOR QUESTIONS

Related, but logically prior to the question I am asking are two other questions: Why should evangelical or conservative religion persist at all, contrary to secularization theory and probably most theories of social change? Whatever the answer, there is reason to suppose it fits both Britain and the United States. Thus, with Bryan Wilson (1985) we might point to the greatly reduced *public* or *sovereign* role religion *can* play in modern society, which thereby allows considerable flexibility in the *private* beliefs, including conservative religious beliefs, persons may hold. This situation obtains equally in both societies, however, and does little in answering the question of why, in America, these conservative beliefs have become politicized in recent decades.

The second logically prior question gets closer to our issue: Why is conservative religion stronger and more popular, more central, in America than in Britain? If "strength" or "popularity" is related to political involvement, regardless of which direction the causal relationship might run, then the answer to this second question would at least bear on the issue before us, if only indirectly. Conservative Protestantism in the United States may be capable of turning political *because* of its strength or centrality, or contrarily, it may gain in strength or centrality *because* it is political. But in neither case do we learn why evangelicalism in America grew politically muscular in the late 1970s. That is to say, the reasons for the greater degree of conservative religion in the United States than in Great Britain, as interesting and profound as they are, are only tangential to the question this essay seeks to answer.

And yet we need to rehearse these reasons because of their relevance for what is to come. Fortunately, several clear answers can be given to the question of why evangelical religion is stronger and more popular in the United States.

CONSERVATIVE PROTESTANTISM IN THE UNITED STATES AND GREAT BRITAIN

David Martin, in an essay published first in *Daedalus* in 1982, pointed out that almost all religious expressions appear proportionately larger in America than in Britain. I might add that even the well-known English fascination with spiritualism and seance may be surpassed by American believers, as we learn from a sample survey of U.S. adults that a quarter of them report having had an experience of clairvoyance; 30 percent, some contact with the dead (McCready and Greeley, 1976, p. 132). Whatever the truth of this point, however, the church membership and attendance of Americans exceed those of the British, so it is hardly surprising to find more American evangelicals as well.

A second reason Martin offered for the greater presence of evangelical religion in the United States is the greater freedom evangelical (or any) religion has had in America because of the absence of a state church and the greater degree therefore of pluralism and voluntarism in the church realm. This difference in degree is nicely conveyed by the existence of the English term *Nonconformist* to describe non-Anglican Protestants; it is a term not found on the American ecclesiastical scene. What is there not to conform to?

A third reason Martin gave is less clear than the first and second, but it is an insight I wish to develop later, so I want to mention it now. Martin pointed to the relationship between the popularity of conservative or evangelical religion and the kind of "political culture" a society has. Noting the degree to which "state provision" (or welfare), formal manners, and a strong labor party are found together, he observed that in Britain this bundle of attributes is high and evangelical religion is low. By contrast, in the United States where evangelicalism is high, this bundle of attributes is low. Formal manners, for example, are replaced by "sincerity," a feature of some importance, needless to say, in a culture that places a premium on religious *experience*. I will say more about this point later.

To these reasons can be added a few more offered by George Marsden in another paper dealing with the Anglo-American comparison (1977). Two of these reasons are clearly cultural in character. One is the importance in American (but not British) thought of "common sense realism," a kind of low-level enlightenment that lends so much pragmatism to Yankee undertakings. The other, in apparent contradiction with the first, is the larger role played by Calvinism in American evangelicalism, and thus the larger role played by intellectual assent to doctrine. It has been, of course, the simultaneous presence of both of these cultural themes that helps to explain the endless sectarian splits in American religion. Doctrine plays a huge role, but doctrinal truth is as plain as the nose on one's face, so one person's judgment is as good as the next person's.

Marsden suggested a third reason, however, which is not cultural but structural: pointing to the more "centralized" communications network in Britain, including its religious network, which makes intellectual deviance difficult to sustain against agreed-upon standards. ("Centralized" is in quotes to distinguish it from the quite different concept of centrality.) The immediate issue he addressed in suggesting this reason has to do with why, for example, there has been no militant creationist movement in England, corresponding to that in the United States. But it seems obvious that this explanation is vastly generalizeable; all kinds of deviant pockets of thought and culture can not only exist but *thrive* in the anonymity of the American social structure. Indeed California, for example, has been described as a collection of just such pockets, united only by a crowded freeway system.

POLITICIZED EVANGELICALISM

This matter of the "centralized" nature of British society is also the explanation Steve Bruce (1983) gave for why no Moral Majority arose in

Great Britain. Because the question of why no Moral Majority exists in Britain, in some sense, is the question of why evangelicalism is politicized in the United States, I want next to review this explanation—not to disagree with it but rather to create a foil with which to compare my own explanation, yet to come.

Actually, Bruce offered a number of reasons for the absence of a Moral Majority in Britain, but, as he said (private letter) just before the publication of his little book *One Nation Under God?* "most of them come down to centralization." For example, in Great Britain *all* political candidates are *party* candidates, which largely immunizes parliament members from the idiosyncrasies of a local population. Special interest groups, which have come to be called *PACs* in the United States (an abbreviation of *political action committees*) thus face a formidable task in British political life. This feature, coupled with the fewer offices filled by election, means that the political agenda is more restricted than in America. Similarly, the media in Britain are "centralized" and, even where they are not state operated, fashion themselves to be serving a *national* clientele to a far greater extent than do their American counterparts. Another way to make Bruce's point is to say that, whereas Great Britain necessarily has a hinterland, it is of far less importance— with far less chance of influencing the core—than is the case in the United States.

The reason that Marsden gave for the modest size of British evangelicalism is thus the same reason Bruce gave for the *non*political nature of British evangelicalism in comparison with politicized American evangelicalism. As I said before, I have no quarrel with any of these arguments. But I *would* point out a missing term in the equation if one reverses the question. Has the United States in the last two decades become significantly more evangelical, and has that evangelicalism become significantly more political, simply *because* America is "decentralized" in its politics and in its mass media? Obviously not. Even if "decentralization" is key to an understanding of the issue, we nevertheless require at least one more element to explain why the changes occurred in recent years. Put differently, "centralization" may be both necessary and sufficient to explain the *absence* of political evangelicalism in Great Britain, but its obverse would appear to be only necessary, not sufficient, to explain the *presence* of political evangelicalism in America. That is why we need to work our way back to David Martin's idea of "political culture" to arrive at a fuller explanation.

POLITICAL EVANGELICALISM
IN THE UNITED STATES

From at least the time of Tocqueville's observations of democracy in America, the "centralizing" tendency, the centripetal force, of American politics has been noted. This is not the same "centralization" as is found in education, the mass media, and intellectual life at the structural level in Britain. Rather, it is the tendency toward homogeneous political outcomes irrespective of politicians' ideology or motivation. One encounters some variety in the rhetoric of U.S. politicians, of course, but seldom in their actions. Even politicians on the extreme, whether on the right or left extreme, are drawn, by the nature of U.S. political life, toward the center. Thus, during the week following the 1984 Presidential election, an election filled with bitter debate and won decisively by the most ideological candidate of this century, Reagan's campaign manager was asked what he thought the President's mandate was. His reply? To reduce the deficit and achieve an arms control agreement. A certain irony lies in recognizing that that answer is the same answer Mondale's manager would have given had Mondale won. The fact that Democrats remained in control of most city, county, and state governments, claimed two-thirds of the governships, plus a majority in the House of Representatives, and increased their number in the Senate only underscores the point: Reagan's victory was a *personal* triumph with voters, but *politically* the nation moved hardly at all.

One might then say that, in America, partisan politics is not an effective way to accomplish political goals. That is to say, the institutions of U.S. politics are so likely to render unchanging outcomes that anyone desiring real change is almost compelled to go outside party channels; hence the periodic outbreak of amateurism in American politics. *But hence also the tendency of social, moral, and thus political aims to be pursued religiously.* This is a two-step argument, and Irving Howe, recalling his life in the 1930s, expressed both steps. He wrote: "If there had been a political movement in America with which democratic radicals could align themselves, even one so unglamorous as the British Labor Party, many of us would have been glad to do so" (1982, p. 286). But he also noted that "our political sects have withered while the religious ones have flourished" (p. 37).

The picture I am offering contradicts the more usual picture of religion and politics in the Western World. The usual picture is that, at least in the nineteenth and twentieth centuries, working-class dissatisfaction has been channeled not into religion but into radical politics. I am suggesting that, in the United States, that is not what happens. Left-wing, but also right-wing, sentiment finds outlet, when it does, not in politics but in religion. One might construe this substitution as merely the Marxian perspective brought up to date; but, if so, we leave unanswered the question of why the substitution takes place in the United States but not in Great Britain. I suggest, instead, that the difference in political cultures sheds more light on this issue.

So far, we have been developing three related generalizations. The first is that, comparatively speaking, British society is "centralized" whereas American society is "decentralized." The second is that this difference shows up politically, so that moral sentiment in Britain, whether of the Left or of the Right, can more readily be expressed through partisan channels, whereas in the United States moral sentiment channeled politically tends to end up being expressed homogeneously, a convergence toward the political mean, if you will. The third generalization, though not quite a syllogistic conclusion, nonetheless flows out of the first two. It is this: In Great Britain, dissent can be channeled politically but is not easily channeled religiously; in the United States, dissent cannot be channeled politically so is therefore channeled religiously.

What do these three generalizations add up to? Without contradicting Steve Bruce's explanation that there is no British equivalent of the Moral Majority because her society is "centralized," I have added, via David Martin's observations of Anglo-American differences in political culture, a fuller explanation of why, in America, there *was* a Moral Majority, a politicized evangelicalism. If I am correct, the Christian Right in the United States is less a religious phenomenon than a political one.

WHY NOW?

There remains the question of why something like the Moral Majority appeared in the United States *when* it did. Even if one grants that it is a religious channel for expressing dissenting political views, what brought on the desire to express that dissent that started in the 1970s and, even allowing for the demise of the Moral Majority, continues today? I see no reason to disagree with the common theme running through most of the books published in the past twenty years that analyze the New Christian Right (Pierard, 1970; Streiker and Strober, 1972; Hill and Owen, 1982; Liebman and Wuthnow, 1983; Bromley and Shupe, 1984). Generally speaking, those authors found the resurgence of politicized evangelicalism to be a response to the perceived moral breakdown of American society as exemplified in antiwar protests, drug use, rock music, and especially altered family structures through divorce, abortion, illegitimacy, homosexuality, equal rights for women, and children's civil rights. All of these things can be found in America prior to the 1960s, of course, but not until then did a "counterculture" emerge and become institutionalized at various layers in society. It was one thing to know that some people got divorced because their marriages were unhappy, for example, but it became something else to be confronted by an ideology rejecting marriage and promoting single parenthood. It was one thing to know that homosexuality exists but another to see a Gay Caucus at the Democratic Party convention. Abortion carried out illegally in a back alley was one thing; abortion publicly funded and openly advocated as a means of birth control was another.

Some invoke the concept of a "New Class" of persons, involved in one way or another in the "knowledge" industry, to identify the occupational locus of this counterculture. Others employ "secular humanism" to describe its point of view. Whatever label may be most apt, the consensus seems to be that a moral revolution is in process that, since the 1960s, has rather decisively evoked a counterrevolution. This counterrevolution is necessarily political because it earnestly does seek to remake American society, but it is evangelically religious too because traditional partisan, and especially legislative, channels are effectively closed to it. Religion is thus the banner under which otherwise unlikely political goals are pursued. One can note, for example, that virtually none of the Christian Right agenda has been enacted into law, and even when President Reagan provided hope by calling Russia an "evil empire," he dashed that hope by opening up diplomatic talks with the Soviets. More dramatic events ensued, causing further confusion on this front. He advocated prayer in public school but had trouble locating judges who found government sponsorship of such prayer constitutional.

The sentiment is there, in other words, and it is real. And events of the last two decades have helped crystalize it into a movement. But the movement emerges in America clothed in distinctly religious garb. If that religious garb came in more colors than fundamentalist-evangelical it might even attract a majority. Ronald Stockton's survey showed:

support for most Falwell positions but a very negative reaction to Falwell. There are two implications. First, the Falwell phenomenon is greater than and independent of Jerry Falwell. . . . Second, support for Falwell's positions goes far beyond his white evangelical Protestant base and includes Catholics and Mainline Protestants. (1984: mimeo)

SUMMARY AND CONCLUSION

We have seen how, in Great Britain, *religious* dissent is less effective than it is in America because of the greater "centralization" in British society. And we have seen how, in the United States, *political* dissent is less effective than it is in Great Britain because of the centripetal force of American party politics. Religion thus becomes the vehicle by which American political dissent gets expressed. To put it cynically, Jerry Falwell was being used; the primary organizers of the Moral Majority probably did not care a fig for Protestant fundamentalism, but they recognized the futility of using partisan politics and especially the legislative process to legalize their agenda. And so they employ a strategy long used in the United States: the moral crusade couched in the terms of Evangelical Protestantism.

ON COMPARATIVE POLITICAL CULTURE

Perhaps because the cultures of Great Britain and the United States share so much, scholars find it a fascinating task to note their differences. Political culture, as we have seen, is one area in which such differences show up. My argument regarding politicized evangelicalism in the two nations thus bears on an issue of British political culture that has long been debated by political analysts. I refer to the so-called deferential working-class voter, the person who, by all economic and demographic odds ought to vote Labour Party but instead votes Conservative.

Frank Parkin had the perspective most congenial to the analysis here. He wrote:

manual workers do not vote Conservative *because* they are deferential, or *because* they conceive of themselves as middle-class;

rather they have a deferential *and* a middle-class *and* a Conservative outlook when they are isolated from structural positions which provide an alternative normative system from that of the dominant institutional orders of society. (1967, p. 289)

From this perspective, therefore: "Socialist voting in general can be regarded for analytical purposes as a symbolic act of deviance from the dominant values of British capitalist society, whilst Conservative voting may be thought of as a symbolic reaffirmation of such values" (1967, p. 282).

"Deference," then, instead of being a character trait of the British working-class personality, is rather a feature evoked in many voters by the very nature of British culture. As Runciman, who might be surprised to find himself on this side of the "deference" issue, has said, it is "some measure of the Conservative Party's success in projecting itself as the party best fitted to exercise the duties of government" (1966, p. 181).

Notice how parallel is the argument regarding Nonconformist religion in England. Most Free Churchmen, wrote Daniel Jenkins, "seem to have taken it for granted that their future role must simply be that of being junior partners of the Church of England" (1975: pp. 103-104).

What we note in these two observations is precisely the "centralized" nature of British culture. When in doubt, vote Conservative and trust the Church of England. To do otherwise requires a blanket of social support effectively insulating British citizens from the central tendencies pushing on them.

No such central tendencies exist in American culture. It is true that out of the resulting diversity comes a homogenizing process at the structural level of politics, but neither Democrats nor Republicans can lay claim to being the "party best fitted to exercise the duties of government." Neither party enjoys the "natural" loyalty of those whose loyalty is otherwise weakened. And the same can be said about religion. Not for a long time has America been presumptively Protestant.

The political dissenter in Britain, therefore, although going against stacked odds, nevertheless has a dissenter's course to follow politically. Not so in America; *political* dissent is hard to sustain. Instead, Americans dissent *religiously*. "We have had hundreds of left-wing [political] sects in America," wrote Irving Howe, "but they have seldom thrived. When you think about it, this seems odd, since there is a long history of religious sectarianism among us" (1982, p. 37). Well . . . it is not odd. Just as Americans *affirm* their citizenship in religious ways—the argument made so forcefully by Will Herberg (1955) in the 1950s when all the United States seemed politically unified—so do they *dissent* in religious ways. And that is what many have been doing since the 1970s, and as Chapter Three argued, that is what many have been doing since the nation was founded.

Part Three

Religion and Law

6

The Courts and Secular Humanism: How to Misinterpret Church-State Issues

INTRODUCTION

Despite the fact that few Americans admit to being secular humanists, the ideology they allegedly hold is nonetheless blamed for society's ills. "Most of the evils of the world today can be traced to humanism," said Tim LaHaye, a Southern California pastor, in his book *Battle for the Mind*. "It is destroying our culture, families, country—and one day, the entire world." Mel and Norma Gabler of Longview, Texas, agreed. They operate a textbook monitoring service to search out ideas that "undermine patriotism, the free enterprise system, religion, and parental authority." Most textbooks, they told *New York Times* reporter Dena Kleiman in 1981, are written from the perspective of "secular humanism, which permeates every aspect of contemporary society and teaches youngsters to lie, cheat, and steal." Indeed, "Humanism is the religion of public schools," say the Gablers, who therefore refer to public schools as "government seminaries."

Religious conservatives, especially the Evangelical Protestant Right, are most likely to castigate secular humanism. More important to this essay, they are most likely to see secular humanism as a movement *voluntarily adopted* in preference to God's guidance through Christianity. Secular humanism is not merely an abstraction, therefore, but an ideology that, because freely chosen, can be just as freely rejected.

According to the religious right, among those choosing secularism are so-called mainline church leaders: theologians, administrators, and clergy affiliated with the National and World Councils of Churches, for example. Thus, to Francis A. Schaeffer, until late one of evangelicalism's "theoreticians," the large, established denominations were "knocked down like a row of ten pins" by the wave of liberal theology early in this century. "Now if Christians had used their strength at that moment," Schaeffer said in a 1982 lecture, "their influence could have stopped the drift toward the liberal theology in the churches, and it could have stopped the beginning of the slide toward a humanist consensus taking the place of the Judeo-Christian consensus which had been the prevalent consensus previously, and upon which our country was founded."

Secular humanism in this kind of discourse is thus an antireligious replacement for an earlier outlook congenial to religion and productive of good citizens and a moral society. This earlier outlook was broadly Christian, of course, but persons who today invoke the spectre of its secular replacement do not have in mind some earlier idyllic theocracy. Indeed, those most vehement in their dislike of secular humanism are the chief heirs of precisely the antinomian, egalitarian, nonconforming, and sectarian tensions that gave rise to the situation they deplore. It was because of these tensions the American Constitution included certain provisions to assure religious freedom. Far from trying to *promote* secularism, then, the Framers and Ratifiers—the creators of the American blueprint, if you will—wanted to *guarantee* the free play of religion. To call the result "secular humanism"—and to believe, moreover, that it is a perspective voluntarily adopted in preference to some other ideology— is thus seriously to misinterpret the issues of church and state. That misinterpretation is what this essay explores.

THE COURT AS AGENT FOR SECULAR HUMANISM

There can be little doubt that American courts are regarded by many as the chief agent for secular humanistic triumphs. Mainline churches may be blamed as responsible for failing to stop the onslaught in time, but the judicial system—especially the U.S. Supreme Court, and especially its rulings on religion in the public schools—for some years has curdled the blood of those, such as LaHaye and the Gablers, who believe secularism is being installed in place of righteousness in the American culture. Even such a centrist as D. Elton Trueblood, in such a middle-American magazine as *The Saturday Evening Post* (July-August 1983), could write, "The zealots of separation have been most successful in persuading the Supreme Court to ban prayer in our schools."

Of course, the allegedly "persuaded" Justices deny they favor either secular humanism or the decline of religion. The outlawing of state-prescribed prayers, said Justice Black in Engel v. Vitale (1962) does not indicate a "hostility toward religion or toward prayer." A year later Justice Clark, in Abington School District v. Schempp (1963), explicitly denied that, by declaring devotional Bible reading unconstitutional, the Court was encouraging schools to teach "a religion of secularism." And yet many of the Court's religious critics think otherwise. Is it possible, they wonder, that the Constitution writers intended to eliminate from American classrooms the very religious influences they wanted so much to protect? How can it be that a school felt free to sponsor an Evolutionary Biology Club but, until forced by the *Mergens* decision (1989), would not consider sponsoring a Bible Club? Is not secularism being promulgated, at least by default, when public schools feel obliged to leave theism untouched?

Such issues give great anguish to some and, it can be assumed, considerable puzzlement to many more. When the law is interpreted as not permitting assistance to theism, is it not then preferring secularism? Is not the Supreme Court therefore an agent for secular humanism?

As plausible as such a charge may sound, it is nonetheless incorrect. At least three kinds of evidence might he offered in rebuttal. First, the Court has a record of protecting traditional religious interests. Second, the Court has a record of recognizing new religious possibilities, though acknowledging these must be balanced against competing interests. Third, the Court is unfairly accused of promulgating secular humanism, when in fact it is merely employing a neutral language, as it must when balancing competing interests.

THE COURT AS PROTECTOR OF TRADITIONAL RELIGIOUS INTERESTS

Today's critics of the U.S. Supreme Court for its role in religion-in-public-schools decisions would be surprised to realize how recently courts were criticized from the other side: for ignoring, and thus allowing to persist, the de facto establishment of Protestantism in public school education. Granted, such de facto Protestant "establishment" is less common today. Nonetheless, one can see instances where the Court has acted to sustain, even encourage, traditional religious (if not just Protestant) influence:

1. In Pierce v. Society of the Sisters of the Holy Names (1925) the right of churches to operate private, parochial schools was firmly declared. Public schooling could have a religious counterpart.
2. In Cochran v. Louisiana State Board of Education (1930) a state's decision to fund the purchase of textbooks, even when used in parochial schools, was upheld.
3. In Everson v. Board of Education (1947) public funds were approved for providing bus service to children attending parochial schools.
4. In Zorach v. Clauson (1952) the Court allowed public school pupils to receive religious instruction during the school day, provided only that it occur off-campus and involve no public tax money.
5. In Walz v. Tax Commission (1970) the policy of allowing tax-exemption for religious organizations was reaffirmed. Chief Justice Burger took this occasion, moreover, to make explicit the Court's "benevolent neutrality" toward religion:

   The general principle deducible from the First Amendment and all that has been said by the Court is this: that we will not tolerate either governmentally established religion or governmental interference with religion. Short of those expressly proscribed governmental acts there is room for play in the joints productive of a benevolent neutrality which will permit religious exercise to exist without sponsorship and without interference.

6. In Marsh v. Chambers (1983) the Court found constitutional the Nebraska Legislature's employment of a chaplain, doing so on the grounds of "the unambiguous and unbroken history of more than 200 years."

It seems hardly correct, in light of cases like these, and in light of a doctrine of "benevolent neutrality," to charge the Supreme Court therefore with being antireligious or pro-secularist.

THE COURT AS BALANCER OF COMPETING INTERESTS

What the U.S. Supreme Court readily admits to being, however, is the adjudicator of competing interests: the "balancer," if you will, between legitimate concerns that nevertheless have the potential for conflicting with each other. Thus, the free exercise of religion has never been understood as absolute, so considerations of time, place, and manner must be weighed against the presumption of this freedom. One might argue that the Court gave short shrift to Mormons in the nineteenth century in summarily finding polygamy "odious" and therefore illegal, but surely the record in the twentieth century is primarily one of everexpanding rights to exercise religion in diverse ways. Consider just the following cases of the past two decades.

1. In Sherbert v. Verner (1963) a Seventh-Day Adventist was declared eligible for unemployment benefits after she was fired for refusing to work on Saturday, her Sabbath.
2. In Wisconsin v. Yoder (1972) Amish children were permitted to drop out of school after eighth grade, since to continue beyond mastery of basic skills was, to the Amish, to become worldly, thus a danger to faith.
3. In McDaniel v. Paty (1978) a Baptist minister in Tennessee was pronounced eligible to run for public office, thus invalidating a state law prohibiting such clergy involvement.
4. In Thomas v. Review Board of Indiana (1981) a Jehovah's Witness whose job called for him to work on weapons contrary to his conscience, and who thus refused to work and was fired, was upheld in his right to unemployment benefits.
5. In Widmar v. Vincent (1981) a Christian group of students wanting to worship on a University of Missouri campus was declared eligible to use state-owned facilities in the same manner as any other recognized student group.
6. In Mergens v. Board of Education (1989) the public schools of Omaha were told that, if student-interest clubs were allowed

the use of school facilities for after-school meetings, then a student club whose purpose is Bible study could not be denied the same privileges.

Once again, in light of cases like these, it seems incorrect to charge the Supreme Court with being secular or antireligious. It is true, as some legal scholars point out, that the Supreme Court seems to have an easier time upholding religious "liberty" than it does "religion," though the first list (of "protector" cases) ought to be proof enough that the Court is not hostile to religion per se. What the second list of cases suggests, however, is that balancing an individual's right to exercise religion against society's right to restrain that exercise is easier than the parallel judicial task, of balancing the government's right to act benevolently toward religion against the citizenry's right to object to such support. Indeed, since 1970 the Court has applied three tests in deciding whether legislation that may in fact benefit religion, is, at the same time, an "establishment" of religion and thus unconstitutional. The three tests are known as "secular purpose," "primary effect," and "excessive entanglement." Government activity must pass all three tests to be legal.

The "secular purpose" test asks about the legislative intention: Is it to benefit religion as such, or is it to achieve some secular purpose that only coincidentally benefits religion? The "primary effect" test is similar to the secular purpose test, except it asks not about intent but about consequence: is religion either "advanced" or "inhibited" by the government action? If religion is neither advanced nor inhibited, then it is not being "established," and the government action is allowable. Finally if, to ensure that religion is neither advanced nor inhibited, government must monitor, or otherwise get entangled with, religion, then such entanglement may be "excessive" and, if so, indicates an unconstitutional establishment of religion.

The operation of these tests is illustrated in Stone v. Graham (1980), declaring illegal a Kentucky law requiring the posting of the Ten Commandments in every public schoolroom. The Supreme Court said:

> We conclude that Kentucky's statute . . . had no secular legislative purpose,and is therefore unconstitutional. . . . The preeminent purpose for posting the Ten Commandments on schoolroom walls is plainly religious in nature. The Ten Commandments is undeniably a sacred text in the Jewish and Chris-

tian faiths. . . . If the posted copies of the Ten Commandments are to have any effect at all, it will be to induce the school children to read, meditate upon, perhaps to venerate and obey, the Commandments. However desirable this might be as a matter of devotion, it is not a permissible state objective under the Establishment Clause.

The third test of entanglement did not arise in this case, of course, because the government activity was found to be unconstitutional by the two other tests.

In applying the three tests for establishment, the Court can be thought of as weighing or balancing two or more legitimate, but competing, interests. Government, in other words, is expected to act to promote the general welfare, but in doing so it must not show religious favoritism. To do so is to "establish" religion. In a similar balancing maneuver, government must allow religious freedom to the maximum possible without jeopardizing society. To do otherwise is to disallow the "free exercise" of religion. (In 1990, Justice Scalia, writing for the majority in the *Oregon Employment Division v. Smith*, declared that *no* compelling interest need be found in order to deny two Native Americans unemployment benefits after they were fired for using peyote during worship in their church. A legislative effort is underway to reassert the need to justify *any* restriction of free exercise with a compelling interest.)

Now, in this balancing of competing interests, the Court necessarily uses language that is neutral with respect to those interests. One consequence is that, even when it is being "benevolent" to religion, the Court may sound secular. A second consequence, however, is that when it declares some religious practice unconstitutional, its decision is especially vulnerable to misinterpretation. This brings us to the third kind of rebuttal to charges that the legal system promotes secular humanism.

THE COURT AS NECESSARY EMPLOYER OF NEUTRAL LANGUAGE

The U.S. Constitution does not require the Supreme Court to give reasons for its decisions. That it routinely does so, often in elaborate form, is easy to understand, however, if we remember the functions the Court plays. Over and beyond the resolution of particular legal conflicts—this being what the Constitution obliges it to do—the Court, through its decisions, performs at least two other tasks. One of these is to educate society in how similar conflicts might be resolved. In the Anglo-American, common-law tradition, where precedents are so vital in the determination of legality, this function is critically important, obviously. The other function is less obvious. It is to offer reasons for the decisions that even the "losers" will accept as fair. That there remain disgruntled losers only means the Court is not totally successful in fulfilling this function, but it nonetheless would prefer all sides in a dispute to walk away gracefully, convinced that justice had been done. Now, it is because the Court performs these two additional tasks that its decisions necessarily employ neutral language.

It follows, then, that in church-state cases, where one party to the dispute can be conceived to be "pro" religion and another party therefore "anti" religion, the Court's decisions will strive for a language that is *neither* pro nor con. This may not be apparent to pro-religion forces in cases where they are the winners, because they will not care much *why* they won. Where they lose, however, even though the language employed in the decisions will be just as neutral, the Court's reasons can be misinterpreted as hostile to religion and therefore secular. Consider the following instances which, from the pro-religion standpoint, were "lost":

1. In McCollum v. Board of Education (1948) so-called released-time religious instruction in public schools was outlawed as "a utilization of the tax-established and tax-supported public school system to aid religious groups to spread their faith." One could interpret this statement of the Court's reason as objecting to the *spreading of faith*, whereas it is actually objecting to the *utilization of the public school system* for that purpose.
2. In Engel v. Vitale (1962) the Court said "it is no part of the business of government to compose official prayers for any group of the American people." One could interpret this statement as *disdaining prayer*, whereas the real objection is to *government composition* of prayers.

Contrast now the language employed in two cases "won" by the pro-religion forces:

1. In Cochran v. Louisiana State Board (1930) the supplying of free textbooks to all school children, even those in parochial

schools, was upheld. "The schools, however, are not the beneficiaries of these appropriations. . . . The school children and the state alone are." One could interpret this statement as *approving parochial education*, whereas approval is really being given to a *state's spending money to provide textbooks for its youth*.

2. In Zorach v. Clauson (1952) the Court declared constitutional the released-time religious instruction that occurs off-campus and involves no tax money. "There is a suggestion that the system involves the use of coercion to get public school students into religious classrooms. . . . [But the record] tells us that the school authorities are neutral in this regard and do no more than release students whose parents so request." One could interpret this statement as *favoring religious classroom instruction*, whereas it is *neutrality with respect to religious instruction* that is being required.

This last case contains also the kind of gratuitous reasoning the Court tries to avoid—and should—if it is to remain neutral. Justice Douglas, who wrote the opinion in Zorach v. Clauson, went on to add the unnecessary reason that "We are a religious people whose institutions presuppose a Supreme Being." Cynics believe Douglas was motivated in this superfluous emendation because it was 1952, and he was angling for the Presidential nomination of the Democratic Party. Whatever the truth of this charge, the gratuitous comment has since been overruled in conscientious objection cases, for example, which find unnecessary the belief in a Supreme Being to qualify for conscientious objector status. One's good standing as a citizen entitled to protection of religious conscience does not, in other words, depend on having one's conscience informed by a Supreme Being theology. The Court tries to be neutral in such religious matters.

A LOOK BACKWARD

We can assume that the legal system of America has regularly tried to maintain this neutrality. What clearly changes, however, is the religious makeup of American society and thus both the nature of the cases being litigated and the sensitivity judges have (or are led to have) toward religious questions. Thus, what neutrality *is* undergoes change. Such change can be demonstrated by contrasting the present situation with a "school prayer" case that arose in Georgia and was decided in 1922 by the Georgia Supreme Court in Wilkerson v. Rome.

The city of Rome, Georgia, passed an ordinance requiring public school principals to see that each school day open with exercises involving a prayer to God and the reading of some portion of the King James version of the Bible. Suit was brought by some citizens who contended that such an ordinance was prohibited by three provisions of the Georgia Constitution: (1) the right of all to worship "according to conscience," (2) the assurance that no citizen of the state will be "molested in person or property" because of "religious opinions," and (3) the declaration that no public tax money will "directly or indirectly" aid any religious groups or "any sectarian institution."

The state's Supreme Court heard the case and pronounced the religious exercises constitutional. Justice Gilbert wrote the opinion (with which only one Court member disagreed), and it is, in retrospect, a remarkable—and remarkably lucid—document. We therefore can learn much, seven decades later, from a close look at the reasoning employed, first by the majority, then by the lone dissenter.

Judge Gilbert began by noting the resemblance between Georgia's constitutional provisions regarding religion and those of other states and of the nation. He then cited a Massachusetts case from 1859 that disallowed "sectarian" objection to such public school exercises as Bible reading. "Those who drafted and adopted our Constitution could [likewise] never have intended it to meet such narrow and sectarian views. That section of the Constitution was clearly intended for higher and nobler purposes . . . the protection of all religions—the Buddhist and the Brahmin, the Pagan and the Jew, the Christian and the Turk." Clearly diversity must be protected, but not "sectarianism."

Something is amiss here to the modern reader. How could one harmonize: (1) refusal to recognize, as "sectarian," a conscientious objection to devotional reading of the King James Bible with (2) support of the "nobler" purpose of protecting religious diversity? A first clue to Gilbert's reasoning comes in his quoting positively from a legal scholar who said that "Christianity is the only religion known to American law." Therefore, like the U.S. Constitution, the Georgia Constitution "never intended to declare the policy of this state to be unreligious or unchristian. This easy equation of "religion" with "Christian religion" helps explain Gilbert's inability to see anything objectionable in public school devotions, even as he safeguards religious diversity, for nobody suffers interference with the "dictates of his own conscience." "The mere listening to the reading of an extract from the Bible and a brief prayer . . . would seem remote from such interference."

How, then, does he handle the charge that such religious exercises, state sponsored and supported, specify the King James Bible and are therefore "sectarian"? Not so, says Gilbert. First of all, differences between the Douai (Roman Catholic) and King James translations, or between the "Rabbinical and Christian editions," are "not known to the ordinary lay reader" and therefore insignificant in the view of the law. Second, although it is true that teachers lead the exercises, and teachers are paid from state taxes, "no theological doctrines are required to be taught. The creed of no sect must be affirmed or denied. . . . No one is required to believe, or punished for disbelief, either in its [the Bible's] inspiration or want of inspiration, in the fidelity of the translation or its accuracy, or in any set of doctrines deducible or not deducible therefrom."

Something is still missing, however, for the modern, jurisprudentially alert reader. What keeps the devotional use of the King James from being "sectarian"? The answer for Gilbert lies in the "real object" of the First Amendment to the U.S. Constitution, which is "to exclude all rivalry among Christian sects." Thus, to assert a difference between the Roman Catholic and King James versions of the Bible "only shows, at the most, that the King James Bible is non-Roman Catholic, not that it is, of itself and necessarily in a constitutional sense, anti-Roman Catholic." Similarly, the Jew may not demand exclusion of Bible reading or instruction in the Christian religion "merely because it is the Bible or the Christian religion." The Jew may seek relief in the law not as a Jew, in other words, but "as a taxpayer just exactly when, and only when, a Christian may complain to a court as a taxpayer, i.e., when the legislature authorizes such reading of the Bible or such instruction in the Christian religion . . . as gives one Christian sect a preference over others."

CONCLUSION

It is perhaps a measure of our constitutional sophistication that such a judicial decision, just seven decades old, sounds so hopelessly insensitive to the demands of justice in a religiously plural society. One can hardly imagine Justice Gilbert's decision today. Even in 1922, Justice Hines of the Georgia Supreme Court dissented. He believed the Rome public school exercises to be illegal on all three constitutional grounds brought by the plaintiffs: (1) Religious freedom includes the right not to worship at all, he said, and yet here the city is requiring "a system of worship for the schools of Rome." (2) To be free of "molestation" for one's "religious opinions" is to be free of "anything which vexes, worries, or disturbs a person in body, mind, or soul," but surely required reading from the Protestant Bible "offends and molests the Catholics and the Jews." (3) Finally, giving public school approval solely to the King James version "discriminates in favor of and aids the Protestant sects," but public schools are supported by taxation from all, and thus the practice is unconstitutional.

Nothing suggests that the dissenting Justice Hines saw himself as a secular humanist or his dissent as antireligious. So it is with his judicial successors, whose positions today are the law of the land. Indeed, as we saw earlier, those insisting on a neutral stance toward all religions in today's America actually claim to be "benevolently" neutral. Certainly it is not the case, as their critics charge, that a position of neutrality necessarily fosters "secularism." To insist that creation science be ruled out of the biology curriculum of public schools, for example, is *not* to elevate evolution to a metaphysical or religious construct that then replaces a Genesis account of creation. Where such construction *is* taught, it clearly is not only unscientific but unconstitutional as well.

Persons unhappy with Supreme Court rulings on church-state matters continue in their charges of secular humanism, however. That they persist in the face of repeated denials by the justices themselves, as well as ample evidence to the contrary, evidence such as we have just reviewed, suggests some confusion on their part as to the real target of their indignation. They attack the Court for promulgating secular humanism, when in fact what they want is what Justice Gilbert of Georgia erroneously believed still existed in this nation in 1922: an avowedly Christian America. But Gilbert misinterpreted the situation then, and today's church-state discontents are even further off-target.

Perhaps nothing indicates the misinterpretation better than the latest effort to countermand the "secular" Supreme Court's position on prayer in public schools. Having tried in vain to enact legislation declaring this nation to be "Christian" and to change the Court's prayer rulings, the evangelical Right now attempts to amend the U.S. Constitution. In its entirety the Amendment reads:

> Nothing in this Constitution shall be construed to prohibit individual or group prayer in public schools or other public insti-

tutions. No person shall be required by the United States or any state to participate in prayer. Nor shall the United States or any state compose the words of any prayer to be said in public schools.

There is an exquisite irony here. The second sentence of the proposal has long been recognized as the law of the land. The third has been explicitly the law since 1962 when the Court outlawed the New York's Regents Prayer in Engel v. Vitale. That leaves the first sentence. What does it make legal that is illegal now? The answer probably is: nothing. Religious free exercise, as we saw, has never been a license to do anything; government has routinely reserved the right to regulate time, place, and manner. What then prevents an "individual or group" from praying in public school today? Very likely nothing, providing only that such prayer: (1)not be disruptive, and (2) not be sponsored by any level of government.

Inasmuch as the evangelical Right already is aware of the first provision—nothing prohibits a student now from offering grace before lunch in the school cafeteria, for example, silently to himself or unobtrusively aloud with others—one must suppose it is the second provision that is to be leap-frogged by this proposed amendment. It is, implicitly, government *sponsorship* the amendment's supporters desire. But sponsorship of "individual or group prayer"? That is precisely what would violate the"benevolent neutrality" the Court has so painstakingly sought to enunciate; it would be preferring a Judaic-Christian style of worship over, say, the meditating-chanting-fasting style of Eastern religions. But America is not *now* a Judaic-Christian nation, whatever it once might have been.

Though not a Judaic-Christian nation, however, neither can it be said to worship secular humanism. Certainly there is no "ideology" of secularism among judges who voluntarily select it in preference to Christianity. At most, one might refer to the "secular" outcomes of church-state issues raised by the facts of religious pluralism and resolved by the Courts in "humane" ways. But that is to say the Courts show no religious favoritism and justify their decisions in language that all citizens are expected to accept. When any group of citizens fails consistently to understand and accept that language, however, it misinterprets the real church-state issues.

7

The Shifting Meaning of a Wall of Separation: Some Notes on Church, State, and Conscience

INTRODUCTION

If a single metaphor dominates American thinking about church and state, it is the metaphor of a wall of separation. Roger Williams in the colonial period, Thomas Jefferson at the time of nation building, Alexis de Tocqueville in the 1830s, and even Supreme Court Justices in the twentieth century have made use of this image: There exists—or ought to exist—a definable barrier with religion on one side, government on the other (see Howe, 1965).

The meaning of this metaphor has clearly shifted through time, however. What each of its preceding employers understood by the image differs, and the understanding by nonspecialists no doubt varies even more. One has reason in the present day to presume even less mutuality of understanding in church-state relations and to regard the wall metaphor, therefore, as essentially meaningless. The 1979 *Annals of the American Academy of Political and Social Science* issue on church and state, for example, suggests this ambiguity by its title, "The Uneasy Boundary." And one scholar goes so far as to charge the U.S. Supreme

Court with rendering decisions diametrically opposed to the original intent of the First Amendment (Malbin, 1978).

At the very least, it can be said the current church-state scene is confused, with many asserting the self-contradictory nature of the two relevant First Amendment clauses; pursuit of "free exercise" of religion necessarily weakens the "no establishment" provision, and vice versa. Thus Catholic parents, who in good conscience send their children to parochial school, see themselves forced by the state to shoulder an added tax because of the way they "exercise" their religion. And persons who, as a religious requirement, would handle poisonous snakes, smoke marijuana, or refuse blood transfusions for their children, regard prohibition of these actions an "establishment" of other people's religion.

The wall metaphor may not be useless for the present day, however, if, instead of seeing random changes in its meaning, we can discern an order to these changes. Put another way, although the "wall of separation between church and state" cannot mean for us what it meant for Jefferson, if we can perceive reasons for its changing meaning, we may be led to a current understanding having continuity, not disjunction, with the past.

THE WALL AS GUARANTEE OF LIBERTY

The first understanding of the wall metaphor in the life of the new nation was as a guarantee of liberty. One searches hard (and unsuccessfully) among the founders and ratifiers for evidence that "religion" was to be kept out of civic affairs, although obviously their opinions varied on how to encourage religion's political contribution without leaning toward ecclesiastical favoritism. The colonists, in other words, were largely agreed on what religion is, even though they were aware of religious differences in their midst. Moreover, despite the fact that most of them were not formally members of any church, these colonists believed religion contributed to the good of society. The reason behind the religious portion of the First Amendment, then, involved primarily a concern for religious freedom.

Surely there can be no debate as to which of the two religion clauses carried the greater clout. Not only did established churches exist in many of the colonies, but some were maintained well into the Federal period. And the historical record shows considerable compromise over how this "no establishment" clause was to be worded, the final rendition referring to laws respecting "an" establishment, not "the" establishment, of religion. In other words, the first Americans knew established religions, had no intention of forcing society to be without them, and apparently were concerned simply that *Congress* not try to regulate them. But why?

If the "no establishment" clause cannot have meant that the framers and ratifiers disapproved of established religion per se, then clearly their greater concern had to do with religion's "free exercise." Indeed, by this reckoning one might almost suppose that the two references to religion in the First Amendment are but a single restriction: Congress shall keep hands off, meaning: (1) it shall not regulate any religious establishments in constituent jurisdictions, and (2) it shall not regulate any of the ways people worship.

Religious freedom, then, seems to have been the paramount—perhaps only—concern at the time, a supposition squaring with the late eighteenth century fact of existing religious pluralism, a history of immigration from religious despotism, and considerable turmoil in prior decades over questions of orthodoxy, church membership tests for citizenship, taxation for church purposes, and so forth. Congress seems to have been saying it recognized the wisdom of a congressional hands-off policy when it comes to religious matters. And it seems to have believed this way because of the importance it attached to the role of religious liberty in maintaining a stable, democratic order.

Indeed, as evidenced by their thoroughly secular enterprise of setting up a federal government, the framers and ratifiers very likely, whatever their own religious predilections, had little fear of interference by any all-powerful church. They were instead, by the 1780s, more concerned to maintain genuine religious freedom, in the conviction that such was necessary for a virtuous republic.

The primary question thus seems to have been, how, in light of past religious restrictions here and elsewhere, often abetted by government, can we try to secure freedom from such restrictions and thus assure a healthy commonwealth? Answer, we shall keep the federal government out of religion, by keeping it both from entanglement with any current religious institutions and from dictating how any religion is to be expressed. There will be, so to speak, a wall to separate government from interfering with the church.[1] In turn, this understanding rested on two unquestioned assumptions: (1) the exercise of religion is necessary to good government, and (2) religion is exercised in a church.

THE WALL AS A BARRIER BETWEEN TWO THINGS

Enlightenment philosophy, combined with the "disestablishment" effects of the First Great Awakening, had enabled the framers and ratifiers of the First Amendment to conceive of this "hands off" policy of religious liberty. Only in a certain sense could they be said to have desired the "separation" of church and state, however. In their basic agreement that "religion" meant "church," and that furthermore it did not matter finally *how* one was religious, the founders of the American government clearly favored the idea of churches. Indeed, they could hardly imagine society without them. Far from wanting government separated from churches, then, they wanted simply to prohibit congressional preference for one church, or restrictions on any.

What, therefore, accounts for a shift in the nineteenth century to an understanding of the wall metaphor as a barrier keeping two entities apart? Part of the answer at least lies in the religious movement called the Second Great Awakening, the evangelical fervor that flowed over much of the United States during the period 1800-1830. Although the first great revival, more than a half-century earlier, had eroded the formal authority of the church and thus helped give rise to the policy of religious liberty, the second revival greatly expanded the church. In this expansion the church's formal authority was not thereby restored, but its intrusion potential was rather suddenly enlarged. As Mathews says:

> The old church had been an organic part of traditional society with a small membership and no orientation toward a goal. Rather it was occupied with maintaining spiritual and moral order. With the advent of the evangelical itinerants, however, there was beginning to develop a new conception of the church as a society of people dedicated to changing their own lives and, by recruitment, those of their neighbors. With this new idea...began a social movement. (1960, p. 36)

This social movement's intrusion potential took a peculiar form, however. Instead of interreligious competition for government favor, a situation probably discouraged by the government's "hands-off" policy, there developed a "voluntaristic principle" and with it a heightened concern for religious minorities. As Lipset has pointed out with reference, for example, to Sabbath laws and religious education in public schools (1963, p. 164), as early as 1810 Americans were used to hearing that Episcopalian, Baptist, Unitarian, Quaker, even the "denier of all creeds," could meet on common ground, and all were equal.

This was the situation encountered by Tocqueville, who visited America in 1831. It clearly struck him with great force. For instance, speaking of American clergy (including many Catholics, incidentally) he wrote, "I found that they all agreed with each other except about details." Then he added: "All thought that the main reason for the quiet sway of religion over their country was the complete separation of church and state. I have no hesitation in stating that throughout my stay in America I met nobody, lay or cleric, who did not agree about that" (Tocqueville, 1969: p. 295).

Of course, what Tocqueville's informants meant by the "separation" metaphor may still have had more to do with religious liberty than it did a "wall" to keep church and state apart. Nevertheless, by the time of Tocqueville's visit, the phrase "separation of church and state" was obviously in common use, and by the twentieth century it had become the dominating image when church and state matters were discussed. Again, why this change?

Among other developments from the Second Great Awakening (and its spillover effect of voluntarism) were a number of sects and cults, many of which were so bizarre as to call into question the policy of religious liberty. From the Transcendentalists to the Adventist, from spiritualism to the Shakers, from Noyes's Oneida to Mormonism—all served to challenge the agreement on what religion *is*. The Revival obviously broke the definitional boundaries around sacred matters, but it therefore posed profound problems when invoking the First Amendment. Speech, assembly, and press were not noticeably forced into redefinition, but religion was.

The other assumption underlying the "religious liberty" interpretation of the wall metaphor was also crumbling. It was, remember, that religion is a good thing because it contributes to the virtuous society. Not only were some of the sects and cults of the nineteenth century doubted as religion; so, too, were they doubted as "contributions" to virtue. Thus, satanic motives were imputed, prophets tarred and feathered, and not a few believers killed (Davis, 1960). The benign belief in religious liberty was undergoing severe challenge.

Quite independent of the Second Great Awakening, moreover, was another nineteenth century force with enormous implications for church and state separation and thus for its metaphoric understanding as well; this force also helped crumble assumptions. Reference, of course, is to massive immigration, especially of Catholics. Was not

Catholicism dedicated to religion's establishment, and did that not mean denominations dedicated to disestablishment must be on guard? Efforts were made to see that Catholics, who would ask special favors of government, did not receive preferred treatment. There must be a wall of separation between church and state.

The pair of assumptions making religious liberty the underlying image of the wall metaphor in church-state relations at the close of the eighteenth century were, by the close of the nineteenth therefore, no longer tenable. The Mormon polygamy case (*Reynolds* v. *United States* 98 U.S. 145 [1878]) perhaps symbolized best that free exercise was limited; no one before had made such "odious" claims in the name of religion, thus forcing the issue. Genuine confusion over "no establishment," by contrast, did not become apparent until well into the twentieth century. When it did become apparent, however, it forced recognition that everyone does *not* regard all religion as a good thing, does *not* believe civil instruction requires spiritual instruction, or that church-sponsored schools deserve government help. The set of "establishment" cases, beginning with *Pierce* v. *Society of Sisters* (268 U.S. 510 [1925]), recognizing the right of parochial schools to exist, began the litigation that continues today, leading to the current three-pronged rule for distinguishing legal from illegal government "support" of religion.[2]

When Justice Hugo Black thus wrote (in *Everson* v. *Board of Education* 330 U.S. 15 [1947]) that government cannot "pass laws which aid one religion, aid all religions, or prefer one religion over another," he was, in all but the final phrase, violating the taken-for-granted world of the eighteenth-century framers and ratifiers. Their assumptions could not be his; Americans now disagreed that religion is good; indeed, as we shall see, they even came to disagree on what religion is.

The result was a First Amendment understanding quite at odds with a notion of a wall to ensure religious liberty. Instead, the metaphor conveyed a barrier image; it was a keeper of peace between factions inclined to entangle, a guardian of separate institutional spheres.

THE WALL AS PROTECTOR OF CONSCIENCE RIGHTLY UNDERSTOOD

And so we have the present situation, ambiguous in the extreme. Cushing Strout, reflecting on what Tocqueville might think were he to visit America now, said:

Increasingly, Americans are facing the conflicts in their own society that new recognition of a radical pluralism of belief has brought about. Just how the state and its agencies should be ordered with respect to a society in which religionists, agnostics, and atheists are seen as spokesmen for legitimate options is a historic issue bristling with controversy (Strout, 1974, p. xii).

Would some new interpretation of the wall metaphor be helpful in resolving this controversy? The wall as guarantor of religious liberty was eroded by doubt about whether religion is necessarily benevolent. Now we see that the wall as barrier has been eroded as well by doubt as to what religion is. The question becomes, then, whether a new image of the wall can fit both the present circumstances and the historic thrust of the First Amendment. Is there a new understanding of separation of church and state that has, at the same time, continuity with the past?

The answer may lie in conceiving of the metaphor as a wall protecting "conscience rightly understood." Use of the term *conscience* implies any profoundly held conviction, whether or not worded theologically or even supernaturally. And use of the qualifying phrase *rightly understood* implies that not all conscientious claims have equal standing.

Invoking such an image gets around the two dilemmas just discussed: disagreement on what religion is, and on whether religion is a good thing. Determining whether someone's action is "conscientiously" grounded may be difficult, of course, but at least it is not complicated by having to judge religious from nonreligious convictions. And, whereas asking whether conscience is "rightly understood" hardly avoids a social judgment, at least it addresses the question forthrightly and does not get mixed up with the related (but confounding) issue of whether conscience embodied in a religious organization is therefore entitled to special consideration. It would *not* be; like the supernatural conscientious claim, it would enjoy no preference over its nonsupernatural counterpart.

What, then, is conscience "rightly understood"? Allusion, of course, is to Tocqueville and his frequent phrase in *Democracy in America*, "self-interest rightly understood." For Tocqueville the qualifier meant a civil awareness, a public spiritedness, a readiness for self-sacrifice. It referred not to forces countering self-interest but to self-interest that took into account its social context. Self-interest in the short run might dictate one course, but self-interest in the long run, recognizing that the collectivity also has interests, might dictate another course and thus be self-interest rightly understood.

Admittedly, "rightly understood" may be as difficult to apply in concrete cases as is the idea of "conscience." Nonetheless, the doctrine in principle is clear: Claims on the grounds of conscience receive special treatment, and, among those claims, those with benevolent civil effect are preferred.

Ironically, this interpretation of church-state may come closer to the House of Representatives' first effort at writing the First Amendment. Following James Madison's earlier wording, New Hampshire's Samuel Livermore offered: "Congress shall make no laws touching religion, or infringing the rights of conscience." Fisher Ames of Massachusetts changed it to "Congress shall make no law establishing religion, or to prevent the free exercise thereof, or to infringe the rights of conscience" (Malbin, 1978). For reasons lost to history, the Senate rejected both of these proposals, and a joint conference of the two houses emerged with the current wording, which, as everyone knows, invites a dual interpretation because of the two clauses: "no establishment" and "free exercise."

Had earlier wording been retained, it is entirely plausible that the current confusion, even contradictory decisions, with respect to church and state might have been avoided. Congress would not have been "neutral" when it came to conscience, as it has had to be when it came to religion, but in recognizing that some claims of conscience are preferred over others, neither would it have been "establishing" any particular religion. After all, the framers and ratifiers had never intended for "rights of conscience" to mean behavioral license; it is but a short step to the rest of the provision: exercise of those rights is subject to the test of their civil effect. Conscience must be rightly understood.

As metaphoric understanding, "conscience, rightly understood" is perhaps already in the making, as least with respect to free exercise interpretations. Since 1965 in *United States* v. *Seeger* (380 U.S. 163), in which an agnostic was granted conscientious objector status, the test has been possession of "a sincere and meaningful belief which occupies in the life of its possessor a place parallel to that filled by the God of those admittedly qualifying for the exemption."

The assumption here is that everybody has a conscience, and anybody's conscience may be entitled to protection. Needless to say, membership in a "religious" organization is not proof that conscience has been engaged, but neither does nonmembership imply a nonengaged conscience. *Welsh* v. *United States* (398 U.S. 333) five years later simply extended this nondistinction; conscience can be "purely ethical or moral" and thus not "religious" at all, yet it still qualifies for exemption.[3]

These free exercise cases, measured against the metaphor of the wall not as barrier but as protector of conscience, would have produced similar decisions. So, too, would other free exercise cases in which persons request any "preferred freedom," to evangelize on city streets, for example, or to be exempt from Saturday work or the flag salute. Judges in those cases have already relied, in effect, on a notion of conscience rightly understood when they determine that litigants were sincere and little or no harm ("undue hardship") would follow their actions. The point obviously is that courts have not in actuality granted such preferred freedoms just because they were religious. These cases may have arrived on the docket for that reason, but the courts also looked at the real and presumed consequences of granting exceptions. It is not too cynical to suggest that if half the draftable population claimed conscientious objection status on Seeger or Welsh grounds, for example, the grounds would be cut out from under them.

But where does this situation leave "churches," as distinct from individuals whose claims of conscience are expressed in ecclesiastical language? Does a church have a "conscience," so to speak, a protected area of rights that it enjoys by virtue of being a church, rights going beyond those of other nonprofit organizations? No doubt churches would retain tax-exempt status by virtue of their nonprofit character, but are *additional* privileges theirs: the right to prevent unionization of their employees, for example, or the right of their agents to refuse to answer grand jury questions?

Without knowing *where* the line would be drawn on such issues, we can nevertheless suggest that the *basis* for drawing the line would probably be different if the wall metaphor were to be understood as a protection of conscience. Churches would no doubt sacrifice something of what they now enjoy, but so also could they receive new benefits. They would *not*, for example, be exempt from the regulations of oversight now pertaining to nonreligious charitable organizations; indeed the religious-nonreligious distinction would essentially disappear. But they *would* therefore enjoy the possibility of tax support for those of its programs judged to have secular purpose and secular effect. Thus, just as a church-sponsored hospital can receive state funds for certain activities but not others, so would parochial schools, athletic programs, or lecture series sponsored by churches.

The singularity of religion would thus be relinquished at the organizational level as the price of expanding the notion of religion into conscience at the individual level. Anything short of this—to assume that a church is easily and uniformly recognizable, and therefore *its* rights easily adjudicated—leads, as it has in recent decades, to conclusions in which some church is inadvertently "established" to allow someone's "free exercise," or someone else's "free exercise" is denied in the interests of "no establishment."

CONCLUSION

Perhaps not surprisingly, then, the dilemma and contradiction now experienced between the two church-state clauses of the First Amendment would diminish, if not disappear. It is reasonable to assume that the framers and ratifiers saw no contradiction in them, but, as we have tried to show, they lived with much narrower conceptions of religion, church, and state. For better or for worse, our notions of these things are greatly expanded, and the goal of religious freedom is thus not easily perceived, let alone achieved. A wall of separation to keep religious liberty from government infringement had to give way, then, as ideas of religion, church, and state broadened. For a period, we suggest, the wall became a two-way barrier, and the favoring of religion by the state—the intrusion of the church into government, so to speak—was to be avoided as much as state intrusion into the church. Now, however, the wall metaphor as barrier has also crumbled because American society lost agreement even more on what religion is as well as whether "it" is benevolent. Distinctions between orthodoxy and heresy disappeared, and so did the difference between church and nonchurch. Claims in the name of religion or church lost their authority, therefore, but claims of conscience did not disappear. America has had to develop a new understanding of the wall metaphor. "Conscience rightly understood," it is suggested, is such an understanding.

8

Constitutional Faith, Legitimating Myth, and Civil Religion

INTRODUCTION

The previous two chapters were analyses of the judicial system's involvement in religion through its role in church-state affairs. Although the actual "religious" nature of American legal institutions could be inferred in those discussions, the notion that courts, especially the Supreme Court, might exercise a quasi-ecclesiastical role in our political culture was not made explicit. This chapter attempts to do, then, what those chapters did not. It results from an invitation by the American Bar Association's journal, *Law and Social Inquiry*, to reflect on a wonderfully innovative book, *Constitutional Faith*, written by Sanford Levinson, a professor of constitutional law at the University of Texas.

Not so much a book review in the ordinary sense, however, the following essay moves from Levinson's analysis of the possibly "priestly" role of law to an examination of how religion (perhaps especially Liberal Protestantism) is manifested in settings some remove from churches. The transition, needless to say, involves the relationship of religion and political culture.

CONSTITUTIONAL FAITH AND FAITH IN THE CONSTITUTION

All nations, at least all nations maintaining a functioning level of order, have legitimating myths. As with all myths, a national legitimating myth will be understood differently by different people, its "truth status" will vary according to the age, sophistication, and other social differences of its holders, and it will be invoked on some occasions more than others. At one extreme, it will be a myth perhaps more akin to Santa Claus, and thus it will be known by all but the very naive to be imaginary, or at least be understood allegorically.

At the other extreme, however, a legitimating myth can be *true.* That is to say, although it, too, will be understood in different ways by different people, in this case the elite are more likely than commoners to assign nonallegorical status to the myth. The rituals, the shrines, and the folklore may still be more seriously attended by the less sophisticated citizenry, but the myth's doctrines will be the domain chiefly of the professional classes. The latter may not literally believe that God has chosen His people, but they are solemn in their belief that more than fantasy is at stake. They believe themselves to be involved in the sacred realm.

Some legitimating myths become civil religions, therefore, and— for better or worse (or both)—America's legitimating myth is one of those. For most Americans, the civil religion is probably a matter chiefly of heroes, monuments, and some vivid narratives. They may or may not feel proud when the Stars and Stripes are flown, and they may likewise be ambivalent about singing the national anthem. They recognize these as important symbols, nonetheless, just as the idea of being "unAmerican" is very real to them.

If most Americans thus constitute a reasonably faithful, if lukewarm, laity in the "church" of their religion, the theologians of this religion are found primarily in the legal profession and, within that profession, especially among professors of constitutional law. Sanford Levinson is one of this latter group, and he contributes to the civil theological conversation in a book, *Constitutional Faith,*[1] which discusses the role in the American civil religion played by one of its sacred texts: the U.S. Constitution. He wrote of his effort:

> This book is written out of . . . ambivalence[:] . . . where "patriotism," measured as commitment to constitutional ideas, strug-

gles against a wariness about a too-eager willingness to celebrate one's own country, including the celebration of its Constitution. The book is intended to make clearer the ambiguities
of "constitutional faith," i.e., wholehearted attachment to the
Constitution as the center of one's (and ultimately the nation's)
political life. I write not in the belief that I can resolve these
ambiguities—there will be many more questions than answers
in the pages to come—but out of a conviction that there is an
important conversation to be initiated about what it means to
be "an American" in the late twentieth century. (p. 4)

With these thoughts, Sanford Levinson introduced *Constitutional
Faith*, a book that, especially if we take to heart the author's warning that
we will encounter "more questions than answers," indeed initiates an
important conversation. The topic is ancient, of course: What does citizenship mean? What *should* it mean? The virtue of Levinson's contribution is the way he links some traditional "philosophy-of-law" issues
to other issues that are not typically regarded as "jurisprudential" in
character.

A very clear example is Levinson's discussion of what it means to
"profess" legal education. If it is a lawyer's ethical duty "to encourage
respect for the law and for the courts and the judges thereof," is it not
incumbent on law professors to *believe* that laws, courts, and judges are
worthy of such respect? The infusion in recent years of neo-Marxian
critical theories into legal thought has intensified the historic debate
over the law's ontological status: Does it exist in any sense except as the
will of the human powers that be? Those who answer in the negative,
thus possibly viewing the law as irrelevant at best and as masking rul-
ing-class interest at worst, are legal "nihilists." And, wonders Levinson along with others, is it proper for them to teach in law schools?

Do not respond too fast. Before the answer, either Yes or No, is
given, consider the following implications of the question:

1. If the law is useful only to those in power and may in fact
   obscure the real interests of the proletariat, how are "real interests" and "usefulness" determined?
2. If law professors must indeed believe in the law they profess,
   how are they to know what that law is?
3. How is a law professor's fidelity to the law to be determined?
   And by whom?

4. Whatever may be the *source* of legal change, the *existence* of legal change is undeniable. In what sense, then, may one speak of variations in the "legality" of laws, as one law (or interpretation) replaces another?

5. If one not only may, but *must*, believe in the law to profess law, what can be said about belief in laws that are then found to be "unconstitutional"?

The thread running through all of these implications, of course, is the inevitability of a realm of morality that must exist in some sense independent of what passes for law at any given time. This independent moral realm may itself be subject to change—the view that there exists a set of fixed "natural" laws, which "humanly created" laws should try to reflect, is only one version of this two-realm portrait—but the presumption of a basis for judging how lawful a law is would seem to be inescapable. Even a nihilist must answer the question why nihilism instead of something (else).

It is this inevitability of a moral—shall we say "sacred"?—realm that lies beyond (or alongside) the law that Levinson approached with such verve and innovation; the law and the sacred are inevitably related. Levinson understandably regards his as an essay about "civil religion," therefore; and this feature of his book occupies the following pages. I want first to discuss some implications of his analysis of "Constitutional Faith" in the context of civil religion rhetoric. And, second, because I have a problem with Levinson's use of this rhetoric, even as I find his argument immensely appealing and provocative, I turn to a discussion of several issues his argument raises.

CONSTITUTIONAL FAITH AND CIVIL RELIGION

Individuals and Civil Religion

It is reasonably commonplace in Western thought, infused as it is with "liberal" or "economic" building blocks in its models, to conceive of civil religion as a social contract gone sacred. We must be constantly reminded that such cannot be the case. Emile Durkheim put it most succinctly perhaps in his assertion that every contract contains a non-contractual element. "What governs the governor of a governed order?"

is another way to render this viewpoint. To put it baldly, social life does not and cannot exist by sheer agreement. Most discussions of civil religion can profit from reminders such as these, because most treat civil religion as if it were simply voluntary.

For example, it is perfectly reasonable to wonder what the framers and ratifiers of the U.S. Constitution *thought* they were doing, and a great deal of evidence can be adduced in answering that question, though debate obviously remains regarding many "original intent" features. But it is quite another thing to ask what the founders *were* doing, *did* do, or *have* done. The first question suggests an image of a bunch of individuals who, after debating among themselves, arrived at a workable consensus that individual Americans, ever since, have been free to believe in or not. Of course, this image must in some sense be true, but it is not the whole truth.

The second question conjures up a different image, therefore: one of discerning citizens who, knowing that democratic society rests on republican virtue, sought to articulate, and then state in document form, the rules by which such a society must be governed. Americans ever since have been free to agree or not that what these citizens discerned was wise or meritorious, but they are not free to "disbelieve" it. For what the founders *did* is, in this sense, either true or not; and if it is true, it is true independent of anybody's agreement that it is true. This feature of America's sacred documents is what permits those documents to be elements of a civil religion and not just symbols of patriotism. Patriotism may be created, but religion is *encountered*. Patriotism is willful, and individuals can share in it to varying degrees; religion *exists*, whether or not individuals are aware of it or agree with it.[2]

Civil religions are rare, therefore, because they cannot be merely the fantastic imaginings of a few individuals who get other individuals to agree with them. They are no more that than scientific theories are merely the products of fertile scientific minds. That fanciful and creative genius may be involved in both endeavors is hardly to be doubted, but my point is that something else is also involved: a "reality," which, however imperfectly perceived and articulated, is nonetheless *there*, independent of individuals' perception of it. In a roundabout way, this is the ontological dilemma that even nihilists cannot escape: From what Archimedian point does one get the leverage to argue that nothing has leverage?

But if a civil religion can be said to be in some sense independent of the individuals who may or may not "know" or "agree with" it, surely individuals are crucial to its maintenance, promulgation, and celebration; that is, its *operation*. Of course. Societies do not exist without individual members; things do not get done, even in groups, unless individuals do them. The radical lesson of sociology is not the denial of persons but is instead the less obvious point that there are products of social life that no particular person, nor any particular set of persons, can be said to have produced. The clearest example is probably language, which, we can assume, is of human creation in a certain sense but, at the same time, is not the creation of its current users. Rather, people encounter their language as a given, however much during their lifetimes it may undergo modification through neologisms and so forth. Moreover, although the variation found among the world's languages might be uttered and symbolized, the structuralists make a convincing case that such choice is severely curtailed by rules of grammar, syntax, and so on, which rules must be obeyed if communication is to occur.

Individuals are crucial to the effective operation in the social life of certain important properties of group existence, then, without being the authors of those properties and without their "belief in" those properties being necessary to the existence of those properties. It makes no sense to talk of civil *religion*, I would argue, except as it has these properties. Indeed, I am no longer convinced that *civil religion* is all that useful a term. Certainly when it is used synonymously with patriotism or pride of place or ethnic identity or old school loyalty, there is a danger that a crucial ingredient is being left out that, to me, must be present if the term *civil religion* is to apply. That ingredient is the notion that civil religion exists not because individuals choose to believe but because it is real.[3]

Part of my discomfort disappears if a term such as *legitimating myth* is used in place of civil religion. It is not because the ontological status of a civil religion is clarified by this substitution. It is not, and we shall return later to this problem. But at least a term like *legitimating myth* invites the inquiry not "Do you believe it?" but "How do you understand it?" *This* attribute civil religions *do* share with patriotic myths, pride of place, school loyalty, and so forth. Individual renditions are significantly different in meaning; particular persons can put their own twists on the tale; and persons can consciously choose one interpretation of the myth over another.

Constitutional Faith and the American Legitimating Myth

No one would deny a role to the U.S. Constitution in America's legitimating myth, however it is rendered. As obvious as this assertion is, another important feature of the situation now gets highlighted: The role played by the Constitution in most renditions of the myth is greatly outplayed by the flag, the monuments in Washington, D.C., the national anthem, Paul Revere, Abe Lincoln, and so on, and so forth. Put another way, a central role for the Constitution probably appears only in the myth as rendered by lawyers and other intellectuals. The public may show some interest in wall-hanging replicas of this sacred document but not enough interest, say, to read it. Any reverence exhibited toward the Constitution is largely the preserve therefore of a highly sophisticated class of people, a proposition well illustrated by Levinson's *Constitutional Faith* itself.

Terminological confusion is all too apparent at this point, however. If the American civil religion (i.e., the American legitimating myth) is conceived in one way—for example, my country right or wrong; the flag is sacred; Americans are God's chosen people—then people in greatest agreement with such sentiments are also the least protective of dissent and other civil rights, and the least capable of understanding the legal process by which such rights are secured. That is, they are less likely to understand the Constitution theoretically or revere it in practice.

If, on the other hand, the American civil religion (i.e., the American legitimating myth) is conceived as involving the inalienability of certain rights, and the sanctity of the legal process by which these rights are secured, then people in greatest agreement with such sentiments turn out to be least comfortable using religious language to express those sentiments.

It is here that one of Levinson's many useful analogies is especially applicable, the similarity between the "profess-er" of law and the theology teacher in a seminary. Both must, in some meaningful way, "believe in" what they profess or else the faith communities they represent are being fraudulently served. At the same time, they, knowing better than most that other legal and religious systems exist, also understand that what they profess is not commonly found among the majority. Like Plato's philosopher-kings, they are aware of the cave, but, as Paul Ricoeur would say, they will have adopted a "second naivete." Their faith, so to speak, transcends the faith of those they profess to, certainly of those for whom they profess. In the case of the professor of constitutional law, as in the case of the professor of Hebrew or Christian Bible, this faith must be real, it seems to me, however much it may differ from the "laity's" faith.[4]

I return now to Levinson's central theme and the central theme of this essay: the undeniable religious elements that surround and infuse the ultimate meaning of the U. S. Constitution. I have suggested that care that must be taken in treating that document as a key element in the American civil religion. Key it is to the legal profession, and key it must be therefore to legal educators' rendition of the American legitimating myth. But much else of what, for most people, makes up the American legitimating myth—the rituals, the saints, the shrines, and so on—do *not* play significantly in lawyers' views of things. Levinson's "constitutional faith" is a special case, therefore, which he on occasion forgot. Why? Because the "too-eager willingness to celebrate one's own country," which Levinson of course recognized for what it is, caused him at times to lump the Constitution in with these other trappings of the popular legitimating myth and thus overlook a vital sense in which the Constitution is inescapably religious.

I conclude this section, therefore, by noting simply that in two places Levinson employed the word *chimerical* in relationship to constitutional matters. The first instance occurs in the context of Levinson's discussion of Lincoln's violation of the U. S. Constitution he had sworn to uphold to maintain the "more perfect Union" the Constitution was designed to secure. About this conundrum, Levinson wrote: "to reach consensus about Lincoln would require reaching consensus about the Constitution itself, and it is the argument of this book that the search for any such consensus is chimerical" (p. 141).[5]

Is *chimerical* not misleading here—misleading because it is biased in a treatise that asks what fundamental meaning the Constitution *can* have? If issues central to this question are chimerical, then the question would seem to be answered in advance; the Constitution could mean whatever one's fancy assigns it.

Levinson most assuredly did not take that position, however. My observation, then—"criticism" is too harsh a word—is simply that Levinson's vital analysis of the status of the U. S. Constitution is not aided but instead obscured by being discussed in the civil religion context. It pushed him toward having to regard the Constitution as possibly the product merely of imagination, toward using the word *chimerical* where I think some word like *evanescent* is truer to his argument. We turn now to a discussion of this point.

CIVIL RELIGION AND CONSTITUTIONAL FAITH

Given the generous parameters allowed here, I have so far indulged in speculation about civil religion more than I have "reviewed" Sanford

Levinson's *Constitutional Faith*. He could justly respond that civil religion was not his main concern, was not even a major peg on which his argument hangs. It is I who have emphasized the term and been arbitrary in stipulating how it should be used.

My reasons for such unseemliness are genuine, however. I take very seriously the religious significance of legal systems, the kind of question Levinson addressed in his book. Parenthetically, I have also noted during my brief stints in law schools, as an auditor of several classes and once as a coinstructor, that most law students appear not to engage these questions with any great enthusiasm. The Holmesian proposition that law is what in fact the courts will decide is apparently enough to get their technological juices flowing, making higher viscosity matters less interesting to them. Levinson pressed such matters, however, and as one who has long been in awe of jurisprudence as the place where sacred and profane meet, I want to register my appreciation for the way he engages us in several of these issues. He *is* addressing the civil religious question in creative ways, and my dyspeptic disillusionment with the way most other authors have handled the term does not keep me from admiring Levinson's various assaults on the central question. I have selected two of these for special attention.[6]

The Constitution as Sacred Text

Many have noted the sacredness surrounding the U.S. Constitution, and comparisons with the Bible are often made. The similarity has led some analysts to see this binding document as both symbol and source of an American integrative ideology, assuming that their Bibles are what, at base, hold Jews or Christians together. As I suggested earlier, however, this is unlikely. Veneration of an object such as the Bible or the Constitution may reflect its role as *symbol*, but the sense of togetherness must precede the symbolic role, thus keeping the object from being the *source* of that sense as well. One encounters the sacred, we said; one does not create it.

No better evidence for this point is needed than the religious wars occurring throughout Western history, many of which can be viewed as partly battles over text. Far from being a source of unity, the Bible instead contributed to disunity. In like fashion, then, although the U.S. Constitution might appear to symbolize American unity—and might on certain ceremonial occasions in fact do so—it is, in reality, primarily a source of disunity in the ordinary operation of the law. People have fundamental disagreements about it. As Levinson saw, and used to great advantage in his first chapter, this disunity occurs along two dimensions.

One dimension of disagreement (which Levinson compared with the Protestant-Catholic difference regarding the Bible as text) is whether the Constitution is exclusively the "written text" or includes "unwritten tradition" as well. The second dimension of disagreement (which Levinson also saw as having a Protestant-Catholic parallel regarding ecclesiastical authority) deals with ultimate authority to interpret the text, whether it rests exclusively with the Supreme Court or resides elsewhere as well (such as in individuals who may disagree with the Court's interpretation). Four positions are thus possible, and Levinson provided us with convincing players in each position. Many of the debates concerning the Constitution can, he said, be organized around these positions.

For example, Attorney General Edwin Meese, speaking to the Tulane Law School, took the extreme "Protestant" position: (1) by insisting (with Justice Hugo Black and Frederick Douglass, among others) that the Supreme Court should not "go beyond" the text, and (2) by insisting (with Andrew Jackson and Abraham Lincoln, among others) that the Constitution is not necessarily the same thing as the constitutional law handed down by the Supreme Court (pp. 39 ff.).

There is not the space here, nor probably the need, to identify minutely the other three hermeneutical stances. All Supreme Court Justices, for example, can be assumed to be "Catholic" on the dimension of interpretative authority, but they certainly differ on the dimension of "text only" vs. "text plus." For any "Protestant" Hugo Black there is a "Catholic" Felix Frankfurter.

What difference do these differences make? It must be noted that in the realm of traditional religions, wars of text interpretation have largely subsided (the Sunni-Shi'ite Islamic division being a possible exception), meaning, as Levinson perceived, that religion has become increasingly privatized. Protestants who disagree with their churches' biblical interpretation are free to start their own churches—and do. Catholics who rebel at Papal infallibility are free to drop out—and do— or redefine religious "duty," as American Catholics have so clearly done when it comes to birth control practices. To say that all of this is possible because religion is privatized, however, is to say that public order does not rest on one or another of these religious interpretations.

Religion has lost "sovereignty"; civil affairs go on independent of any-body's view of the Bible, so to speak.[7] Such is not the case with Ameri-cans and the U.S. Constitution, however. At various points in the legal process—to judges certainly, but also to law professors, lawyers, and their clients—just how the Constitution is regarded must be of tremen-dous importance. The law, it might be said, intrudes into public life in America in a way that religious texts do not; ironically then, it has an unavoidable involvement in moral issues and thus a certain link to America's civil life that religion as commonly understood does not.

The Constitution and Morality

In his Chapter Two, therefore, Levinson examined what this link might be. Why, to put it crudely, should the U. S. Constitution *deserve* moral respect? One answer (hereafter Answer One)—the answer associated with Holmes, Frankfurter, and (most recently) Robert Bork—is that the Constitution deserves *no* such respect. "For Holmes, government was a reflection of power, and nothing more" (p. 68). Judges are thus man-dated to assess only the conformity of actions with what the law, Con-stitutional or legislative, says. Any moral intrusion is not to come via judges, then, but via "the initial decisionmaker, whether the constitu-tional framer or the legislator" (p. 81). The Constitution deserves respect as a fundamental set of rules but not as a morally prescient document.

Levinson saw through Answer One, however:

> The obvious problem . . . is how one conceptualizes the "moral-ity" that is supposed to be translated by the judge. . . . Now obviously one might be fearful of an over-readiness of review-ers to substitute their "moralities" for one's own, and one might therefore emphasize to them the necessity of following one ' s "exact instructions," without deviation. But this injunction . . . ultimately makes little sense. The problem is that what counts as the "exact instruction" can be delineated only in light of some complex theory of the writer, including a constructed image of her moral life. (p. 81)

The example Levinson offered is as instructive as it is homely. A mother, who regularly employs a neighbor to care for her son, has become upset at the son's repeated tardiness in being sent home from the neighbor's. The mother therefore writes instructions explicitly directing the neighbor to send the boy home promptly at 5:00 P.M. and "under no circumstances " is this directive to be violated. The next day a tornado descends on the neighborhood just before 5:00, and the boy is kept inside, prevented from venturing home on time. The question is not whether the neighbor misbehaved; presumably no one would assert that. "Rather, we must ask, did the neighbor violate her instructions? That is, did the neighbor violate the law—the mother's instructions—in the name of morality . . . ?" (p. 82). It would seem that some notion like "exact instructions" is illusory; the strict constructionist position is not literally possible.

Alexander Bickel, a Frankfurter clerk and later Yale Law School professor, attempted to resolve the dilemma of this Holmesian position by suggesting that judges can and do absorb the "fundamental values," the "traditions" and "history," of their society and then conservatively reflect back in their decisions these unwritten features of the law.[8] But this formulation, Levinson asserted, "seems to assume . . . that there is a relatively unequivocal American tradition that can be identified and adhered to by persons of good will" (p. 72). He therefore found this answer inadequate.

The second answer possible (hereafter Answer Two) to the question of why the Constitution deserves moral respect starts off sounding radically different from the first. It is that the Constitution is the "guarantor of justice" (p. 68). Neither a synonym for majority rule nor a mere set of procedures, as the first answer would have it, the U.S. Constitution has its own "integrity"; it "has a point" that can be stated:

> The point of American constitutional law in particular is presumably to attain the values summarized in the Preamble and otherwise found within the materials of the American political tradition. (p. 75)

> [It is the] point of the American Constitution, if we are indeed to have any "faith" in its goodness, . . . to achieve a political order worthy of respect, and there is a very heavy burden of proof on any analyst who would say that the Constitution *must* be interpreted in a way that brings it disrespect. (p. 77; emphasis in the original)

But Levinson believed he saw through Answer Two's argument, too. Preamble values cannot be controlling. Why? Or, asked another

way, why is this position "extremely controversial within the legal community?" (p. 78). Because "we live in a radically pluralistic world"
(p. 78). There is no "shared moral reality" uniformly interpreted (p. 78).
The losers of legal dispute who ask for justifications "are often quite
ready to believe that the reasons offered are but ill-disguised imposi-
tions of alien political values held by undisciplined judges" (p. 80).
Preamble values are "chimerical."

But are they really? Is it not rather that they are evanescent,
advancing and receding through time: a "shared moral reality" now
more, now less, revealed in our "history and traditions." Many issues
once legally disputed, for example, are now resolved, if not "forever"
then by lengthy precedents; for example, the government's right to tax
income, to regulate traffic, to control crowds. "Losers" in disputes over
these issues continue to emerge, of course, but they are losers whose
cases are at the "edges" of the law, helping to refine the "point" of justice as our "history and traditions" evolve.

Regarding the question of the Constitution's respectability, then,
Answers One and Two, identified by Levinson as polar responses to the
question, and originating from radically different positions, converge in
an ironic way. Answer One, disclaiming any moral role for judges,
acknowledges that such a role, being nonetheless inescapable, depends
upon judges' fidelity to American history and traditions. Answer Two,
claiming precisely a moral role for judges via the morality inherent in
the Constitution, acknowledges that, although no single moral interpretation is ever going to be permanently available, judges must extract
it by remaining faithful to American history and traditions as they
understand them.

The question I would ask at this point, as might be surmised from
the front half of this essay, has to do with the ontological status of the
phrase *history and traditions* in this equation. Can this phrase refer to
just anything? Is it by chance that in the United States it refers to the
events in colonial America whereby Enlightment thought and covenan-
tal Protestantism converged? Is it merely coincidence that rights of citizenship have moved toward incorporating more, not fewer, persons? Is
it just by popular will that individual rights continue to expand at the
expense of the legitimacy of claims put forward by ascribed groups?
The answer to these and similar questions is negative. These are not
chance trends. Nor has American law been drawn in these directions
simply because of the ballot box. And certainly the voting public does
not merely follow the courts' dictates.[9] Something, which might well

be called *constitutional faith* but could also be conceived as fidelity to American history and traditions, is an independent force in this equation. The linkage of law and morality may be loose, in other words, but it is real. It may be apparent at some times more than other times. It is, as we said, evanescent. But this does not make the linkage—the "civil religion," if one can live with this term, chimerical. Americans, by and large, *are* committed to the symbols of their common faith. If they were not, they would not fight over how the U.S. flag should be treated. As only one of these symbols, however, the Constitution does not so much *unify* Americans morally, therefore, as it provides a vehicle for *expressing* moral unity. That it can—and should—perform this function is a matter of constitutional faith, perhaps, but, more importantly, the Constitution provides limits (granted, evanescent limits) within which American moral unity, to the degree it *exists* at any slice in time, *can* be expressed.

Thus, to take the example used repeatedly to good advantage by Levinson to make other observations, it seems safe to predict that, even were Congress to legalize slavery, and even were Robert Bork magically to find himself Chief Justice, the U.S. Supreme Court would still declare such legislation unconstitutional. Why? Not because public opinion, per se, opposed such legislation; indeed it is hard to imagine enactment of a slavery law unless legislators believed they had the majority backing of their constituents. It is rather because the judiciary, whatever their personal moral sensibilities, could not be so far out of touch with America's "history and traditions" as to once again permit chattel slavery. At least they could not and still have been functioning adequately as judges.

Perhaps this last assertion requires clarification, and perhaps an example will help. As I write this essay, a Texas judge has declared that his light sentencing of the killer of two homosexual "cruisers" was more a product of the unworthiness of the victims than the wantonness of the crime. Needless to say, not just gay interest groups but also other elements of the public committed to justice have risen up. The point here is not whether the judge's opponents "won" and got him to resign (or defeated him in the next election); it is rather that no public opinion formed to defend his eccentric moral reasoning. By contrast, opposition opinion *did* form, in spite of the homophobia known to exist among Americans, maybe even the "majority" of Americans.

Though the short-term result in this case might have been anything, then, some lesson is to be learned from this differential tendency for the public to mobilize. What is to be learned is that "history and traditions" *do* exist in America, and that Americans, *in the long run at least*, are responsive to their appeal. For those who hold Answer One, this was the point that Alexander Bickel was making when he argued that an activist Court should not act while public opinion is still inchoate. But in a way it is the same point made by holders of Answer Two when they acknowledge that no uniform moral reality necessarily exists at any particular moment; the best to be hoped for is a judiciary that is sensitive to America's history and traditions. Moreover this position turns out to be Levinson's:

> For me, signing the Constitution—and agreeing therefore to profess at least a limited constitutional faith—commits me not to closure but only to a process of becoming and to taking responsibility for constructing the political vision toward which I strive, joined, I hope, with others. It is therefore less a series of propositional utterances than a commitment to taking political conversation seriously. (p. 193)

Is this not a declaration of faith in American history and traditions?

An Ironic Convergence

The convergence that I am claiming to see in Answers One and Two— the convergence that Levinson, in identifying his own ambivalent constitutional faith, articulated so well—might be conveyed with reference to the preceding discussion of "Protestant" vs. "Catholic" views of the Constitution. Differing views of the foundational document can be held, as can differing views regarding judicial monopoly of its interpretation. But when it comes to the operation of the law, how much difference do such differing views make? Some perhaps in the alacrity or reluctance with which judges would "engineer" social change. And some perhaps in judges' readiness to overturn earlier decisions. But surely the large answer is found in the constraints put on the law by American history and traditions as reflected in precedents. Neither Protestant nor Catholic can easily kick over those traces. They are there, and Levinson not only saw them but put his faith in them. In effect, he chose the Catholic-Protestant position (among the four positions possible) because this gives law the widest latitude, but he has "faith" that this latitude is constrained by American history and traditions.

A Conclusion

In spite of his declaration of faith, however, Levinson maintained a certain reluctance to admit the step that I think he has taken—and must take, given the nature of things. "I am an unabashed positivist in one important sense," he wrote; "there is no necessary connection between law and morality" (p. 169). I would assert just the opposite about *Constitutional Faith*; it demonstrates eloquently exactly the inextricablity of law and morality. Moreover, it helps us see how the law is not just entangled in moral issues, but also how it is, at least in a religiously plural society like the United States, inevitably an arena for playing out transcendental doctrinal matters as well. If religious institutions as commonly understood have lost sovereignty, in other words, Levinson helps us see how legal institutions have had sovereignty thrust upon them. *Constitutional Faith* is thus a treatise in the tradition Walter Lippmann called the "public philosophy." Oddly enough, the academy during the second half of the twentieth century will probably be found to have paid scant attention to the issues of public philosophy; either they will have been ignored as imponderable, a la the positivists, or else converted to technological questions, which probably amounts to the same thing, operationally speaking.

Levinson, to his credit and in spite of his disclaimer, is an exception to this generalization. His is an earnest contribution to a very serious conversation. Although I have expressed some reservation about his use of the term *civil religion*, I unhesitatingly acknowledge that *Constitutional Faith* addresses matters of profound importance to the public philosophy. It therefore deals with civic issues that must be understood as having religious significance. These remarks should not be read as suggesting anything else.

Part Four

The Trajectory of Religion and Political Culture

9

Religion and the Persistence of Identity

INTRODUCTION

In this and the next two chapters we return to the analysis of religion as it is usually perceived: organized into churches. Unlike the essays of Part One that looked backward in time, or the essays of Part Two that looked at the current scene, these three analyses are efforts to peer into the future. What is likely to happen in the relationship between church and political culture in America?

The present chapter attempts to specify what it means to say that church religion, unlike "jurisprudential" religion, is losing sovereignty, defined in the Preface as the increasing privatization of religion and its moral neutralization. This chapter, by invoking the notion of primary vs. secondary identity, also examines what effect lost sovereignty has on religion's centrality, defined in the Preface in terms of "ritualization" and "commodification." Because this chapter is based on an essay whose origin was a research proposal, and the research has since been carried out, a Coda is added that compares the actual findings with the projection.

Chapter Ten is an exercise in outright forecasting, of what will happen to American church membership rates, and concluding Chapter Eleven focuses on what is likely to happen to American mainstream Protestantism in the next few decades.

A CASE IN POINT

During a summer weekend every year in Santa Barbara, a Greek Festival is held in one of the city parks. The booths selling souvlaki and dolmas are operated by, and for the benefit of, the Greek Orthodox parish in town. And this sponsorship is prominently displayed by a sign on each booth. In 1986 I noted something interesting about those signs. Carefully and beautifully printed, they announced the sponsor as "The Greek Church of Santa Barbara." Then inscribed in longhand, between the words "Greek" and "Church," someone had added "Orthodox." Whoever first prepared the signs, in other words, had failed to mention the part of the label that, in substance, is of greatest importance: What church is sponsoring this booth? The Greek *Orthodox* Church!

Of course, nobody was misled or in doubt. Perhaps only a perverse sociologist of religion would even notice. But I *did* notice, and I was struck by the implication of the original omission. The signmaker, although acknowledging by the choice of words that there could be Greek sponsorship that is *not* the church, was also implying that church-going Greeks in Santa Barbara go to *one church only*.

How characteristic of a disappearing past, I thought to myself—to have one's church more or less dictated by one's primary group allegiances. And not just dictated by, but expressive of, those allegiances. Under these circumstances, the church is surely a vital part of people's identity. Indeed, as I ruminated further, I recalled how William Swatos argued that the American style of denominationalism, and the consequent "religiousness" of the American people, grew out of exactly this capacity of churches to "fit people into the local community" (1981, p. 223). They could organize "communal relationships relating to the transcendent realm in a pluralistic socio-cultural system" (p. 222). The church was one of the ways people knew who they were.

But this social function was strongest in the nineteenth century, as Swatos suggested; in this century, especially since World War II, the church has decreasingly played this "collective-expressive" role, even if exceptions may he found, as the Santa Barbara Greek Festival would suggest. After all, fewer and fewer of us are embedded in primary groups, and—what may be more important—the few primary group ties we still have are not overlapping. Instead, as the classic sociological formulation has it, we are chiefly involved in a series of segmented relationships.

For many therefore—especially those not embedded in primary groups—the church is simply one of these segmented relationships. Far from expressing collective ties, the church is one of the ways by which individuals (often joined by other members of their nuclear families) cope with this segmented life. Very much a voluntary association, the religious organization represents for such people not an inherited relationship but a relationship that can be entered and left with little or no impact on their other relationships. Church, for them, is not simultaneously a gathering of kin, neighbors, fellow workers, and leisure time friends but rather a separate activity, expressing another meaning. This pattern is seen in study after study showing that the persons most involved in churches are the same persons most involved in other organizations as well. (See, e.g., Lazerwitz, 1962; Stark and Glock, 1968). It also indicates how churches have lost sovereignty by becoming increasingly a private matter and therefore neutralized in moral issues over which people disagree.

Does this mean that religion, under these circumstances, has little to do with people's identity? And if, as is frequently said and is probably true, this individual-expressive pattern is replacing the collective-expressive pattern, does this mean that religion is decreasingly involved in people's identity? Such questions are what I explore here.

A NOTE ON THE CONCEPT OF IDENTITY

Hans Mol (1978) is one of those who have reminded us that we use the concept of identity in two quite different ways in the social sciences. The first way of looking at identity suggests the immutable, or at least the slowly changing, core of personality that shows up in all of a person's encounters, irrespective of differing role partners. The second way suggests the transient and changeable self as persons move from one social encounter to another, offering a somewhat different identity, as it were, in each place. The first notion of identity suggests that it is involuntarily held; the second, that it can be put on and off. The first is nourished in primary groups, probably early in life; the second exists precisely because much of life is lived in arenas outside of primary groups.

About these two notions of identity, the following observations might be made: (1) Both notions can be appropriate and therefore useful. (2) Some institutional spheres, most notably the family, are inevitably important in the first sense, whereas other institutional spheres, most notably the workplace, are inevitably important in the second sense without necessarily being important in the first sense. (3) Some institutional spheres, and here I nominate religion but also ethnicity as examples, may, in modern societies, be shifting from being important in the first sense, to being important only in the second sense.

It happens that, though I think this third assertion holds true for both religion and ethnicity, it can be more clearly stated and more readily shown in the case of ethnicity. Indeed, as I will presently suggest, recent debates about ethnic group revival turn out to be debates about a shift in the role ethnicity plays in people's identity. Despite this apparent subject matter, however, my real focus here is not ethnicity but the church. It is their parallelism and close ties historically in America that allows ethnicity to serve as a sort of surrogate for religion in my discussion.

RELIGION AND ETHNICITY

Little doubt exists about the intimate link between religion and ethnicity. Whether the latter is conceived objectively or subjectively, and whether it is measured along the lines of acculturation or assimilation, involvement in the religion characteristic of one's ethnic group is always judged to be powerfully correlated with the strength of one's ethnic identity. (See, e.g., Price, 1963; Gordon, 1964; Lieberson, 1970; Marty, 1972; Sandberg, 1974; Stout, 1975; Miller and Marzik, 1977; Moskos, 1980; Padgett, 1980; Reitz, 1980.) A variant of this perspective is the research showing how different ethnic groups practice a single religion differently. (See, e.g., Greeley, 1971, 1974; Abramson, 1973.)

Despite the undeniability of this relationship, however, a sense of ambiguity about it is readily detected. Timothy Smith (1978) has argued that the religions of immigrant groups in America were not simply additional luggage from the old country, kept as nostalgic reminders and thus defenses against assimilation. Instead, religion played a dynamic role in the very formation of ethnicity as migrants created community in America, where none may have existed before.

Abramson (1980) struggles with the same issue. It is clear, he says, that in some instances—such as the Amish, Hutterites, Mormons, and Jews—ethnicity *equals* religion. That is to say, were it not for religion, the ethnic group would not even exist. In other instances—such as the Greek Orthodox or Dutch Reformed—religion is a powerful foundation of ethnicity but shares this foundational character with a unique territorial origin and very likely a distinctive language as well. In yet other instances—such as Irish, Italian, German, and French Catholicism—the link between ethnicity and religion is real, but religion is not a definitive, only an empirically probable, component of ethnic identity.

It would seem that what is at issue here is not simply the recognition that ethnic and religious identity can vary in *strength*, but that ethnicity and religion can differ in *meaning* as well—and thus in the kind of identity they might provide. Here is where the debate over the authenticity of ethnic "revival" is relevant (and so is the analogous debate over religious revival). So-called straight-line theorists such as Gans (1956) or Steinberg (1981), argue against so-called "cyclicists" such as Hansen 1952) or Novak (1971). Although acknowledging that peoples' ethnic identity may undergo an upsurge, these straight-line theorists also insist that such an upsurge is not a return of an earlier ethnic identity but is instead an alteration in the meaning of ethnicity. In the extreme, they say, it is precisely because ethnicity has lost its structural importance that more and more people can indulge in ethnic leisure-time pursuits. Ethnicity is less important for identity in the first sense, in other words, which allows it to be important for identity in the second sense.

This argument, of course, parallels the one about religion, made most forcefully by Bryan Wilson (1966), that, for example, America only appears to be the most religious nation because in reality it is the most secular. Granted, this rendition goes, church-going rates are high, but only because such choices are voluntary and therefore structurally unimportant; they *mean* something different from involuntary church going.

I submit that these arguments are best understood if, in each case, one side (the cyclicists) is seen to be attributing a single meaning to identity as it relates to ethnicity or religion, whereas the other side is noting the shift in meanings. This second position says, granted ethnicity (or religion) may be regaining importance, but if it is, it no longer provides the same *kind* of identity it used to provide. To put it yet another way, it is because ethnicity has declined in sovereignty that it may increase in centrality.

THE ISSUE GETS SHARPENED

This issue is clearly observable in the literature on religious and ethnic intermarriage. As an empirical generalization, we know that intermarriage rates tend to fluctuate inversely with the availability of homogeneous partners. Thus, Catholics in Raleigh or Little Rock marry non-Catholics at a higher rate than Catholics in El Paso or Providence (Thomas, 1951), and Greek-Americans in the South and West marry non-Greek Americans more frequently than do their fellow ethnics in the North and East (Moskos, 1980). What are we to make of a contrary finding then? Koreans in Hawaii, where they are sizeable in number, out-married in the 1970s at a rate in excess of 80 percent, while Los Angeles Koreans, also numerous, had an intermarriage rate only one-third that size (Kitano et al., 1984).

The explanation is quite simple. Koreans in Los Angeles are a closer-knit group; they exercise greater control over the activities of their children, and provide more ethnic organizations for those children to attend. The fact that a higher proportion of the Los Angeles Koreans are first-generation American than one finds in Hawaii, or the fact that interethnic contact has long been institutionalized in Hawaii, helps explain the greater insularity of the Los Angeles Koreans, of course, but the controlling agent is the insularity, whatever its causes. The empirical generalization regarding sheer numbers of a group and its members' proclivity to out-marry turns out to depend upon the group's meaning to its members. Whether many or few in number, if members' identities are importantly determined in the first of our two senses previously, if their core personalities are shaped by their ethnicity, then we can expect lower intermarriage rates. Correlatively, if intermarriage rates are high, or if other evidence suggests that the ethnic group's insularity is not great, then we can assume that its members' ethnic identity exists chiefly in the second sense: an identity that may be more or less important, depending upon circumstances.[1]

We have already noted about the first kind of identity that it is involuntary—that it is thrust upon its possessor by so many others, in so many circumstances, for such a long time, that, even if one wanted to escape it, one could not. The phenomenon of ethnic "passing" (e.g., of a black as white, a Jew as Gentile), now no longer much noted, illustrated by its poignancy this essentially involuntary character; one chose to discard an identity of the first sort at great social risk, of course, but also at great psychic cost because this was no facade being peeled away but a pulling out of roots.

RELIGION AND IDENTITY

Now, it was Durkheim's great insight that religion is born out of the social circumstances providing those involuntary roots. People are led, he said, to represent their sense of unity in the groups of which they are members: to express that unity in ceremony and symbol, in belief and ritual. In the case of the central Australian aborigines he studied, there was no choice in the matter.

Because modern society so little resembles the Australian outback, and because the religions Durkheim described so little resemble religions of our day, we may too easily dismiss this Durkheimian insight as no longer applicable. Perhaps it is true that society in toto no longer evokes this sense of unity—or, if it does, does so only momentarily. We must recognize, however, that, even in modern society, the church may be an expression of intense primary group ties, especially if those ties are to overlapping groups. That is the possible significance of the Greek Festival, even in Santa Barbara.

At the same time, however, we must also recognize that for others the church is a secondary association, a voluntary activity that is switched on and off. Under these circumstances, the church may be very important to some people, and thus a source of identity for them, but the identity provided will be an identity of the second sort.

TWO VIEWS OF THE CHURCH

We have, then, two contrasting views of the church in contemporary society. On the one hand, there is what I earlier called the "collective-expressive" view, in which involvement is largely involuntary because it emerges out of overlapping primary group ties not easily avoided. On the other hand, there is the "individual-expressive" view, in which involvement is largely voluntary and independent of other social ties. I also implied that the social conditions eroding the first view are the same conditions that permit, perhaps even encourage, the second view. For example, the parents of children in the ghetto who can think of no alternative to the parochial school—because: "What would neighbors think? Where else do schoolmates also contend with English as a second language? Aren't they safer with their own kind?"—will, in due time, produce parents who choose the parochial school—because: "The kids should know how they are different from the neighbors. Where else can they be taught their ancestors' language? Our people have become so spread out, only the parish brings us together." In the first instance, the parents and children have little choice than to be involved in the church; in the second instance, the very forces that free them from mandatory involvement are forces that encourage their voluntary involvement.

Nobody states this theoretical viewpoint regarding religion and identity better than Thomas Luckmann. At one extreme, he says—the extreme at which Durkheim was theorizing—there is congruence among "church, the sacred cosmos, and the hierarchy of meaning in the world view" (1967, p. 79). As a result, public institutions "significantly contribute to the formation of individual consciousness and personality" (p. 97). Once there occurs the "institutional specialization of religion," however, the relationship of the individual to the sacred cosmos and social order is transformed (p. 80):

> In view of this situation it is useful to regard church religiosity in two different perspectives. First, we may view church religiosity as a survival of a traditional social form of religion . . . on the periphery of modern industrial societies [i.e., the collective-expressive view]. Second, we may view church religiosity as one of many manifestations of an emerging, institutionally nonspecialized social form of religion, the difference being that it still occupies a special place . . . because of its historical connections to the traditional . . . model [i.e., the individual-expressive view]. (pp. 100-101)

Indeed in the second of these situations, the individual is alone "in choosing goods and services, friends, marriage partners, neighbors, hobbies, and . . . even 'ultimate' meanings. . . . In a manner of speaking, he is free to construct his own personal identity" (p. 98.).[2]

Luckmann's theory and my explication of it suggest that people can be located on a grid, whose two dimensions are (1) involvement in overlapping primary groups and (2) involvement in secondary groups. Because of the dialectical and inverse relationship between these two dimensions, most persons score as High-Low or Low-High (though obviously cases are found everywhere on the grid.) Church-affiliated people who are High-Low will tend toward collective-expressive involvement in the church, and their religious identity will tend to be of the involuntary, immutable type discussed earlier. By contrast, church-affiliated people who are Low-High will tend toward individual-expressive involvement in the church, and their religious identity will tend to be of the transient, changeable type.[3]

The chief research task obviously involves discovering what primary and secondary group ties people have, and how strong those ties are. It also involves learning whether the strength of those ties is related to any difference in meaning that church involvement has for people, and whether this difference influences their identities. Although the study of voluntary association memberships provides some precedent here in the case of secondary groups, except for the considerable literature on ethnicity and assimilation, we know very little about people's primary ties outside the nuclear family. Yet note the importance attached theoretically to "redemptive institutions" (Nisbet, 1953), "mediating structures" (Berger and Neuhaus, 1977), and, most recently, "communities of memory" (Bellah et al., 1985). Clearly such primary groups are thought to remain important in at least some people's lives— through not just ethnicity but also extended kin groups, work-related collectivities, fraternal or "cultural" organizations, even regional or class allegiances. *Community*, defined as a "network of social relations marked by mutuality and emotional bonds" (Bender, 1978, p. 7), we have to assume, has not entirely disappeared.[4]

I am currently involved in an effort intended to test these ideas. Joining with a few colleagues in various parts of the nation, I hope to receive funding for both a telephone survey and personal interviews, focusing on the now-maturing post-World War II birth cohort, but designed to help in understanding the rather sizeable religious change going on around us. What I have outlined is a theoretical perspective that bears on at least these questions:

1. Why, after decades of growth, have mainline American denominations begun to decline?
2. Why, in the face of undeniably continuing secularization, is orthodox, evangelical religion experiencing new energy?
3. Why has Catholicism in America become a major battleground of the Roman Catholic Church's confrontation with modernity?
4. Why are there such regional variations in American church vitality?

Perhaps even the recent rash of so-called new religious movements also can be placed on the list. In any event, contrary to simple-minded theories of secularization, religion has not disappeared in America even though the church's role has certainly changed. The theory presented here suggests that persons are variously involved in both primary and secondary groups and that these involvements influence not just the meaning the church has for them but also influences their religious identities. Although obviously incapable of explaining everything, this theory is nevertheless offered as a reasonably comprehensive perspective. What evidence thus far supports the theory?

WHAT EVIDENCE THUS FAR SUGGESTS

1. Though rarely analyzed in this fashion, the data on assimilation suggest that the stronger are persons' ethnic ties, the more they remain loyal to the religious organization associated with their ethnic groups (see Reitz, 1980, p. 116).[5] Granted, church involvement can be said, on the basis of this same evidence, to be merely another *indicator* of ethnic identity and not necessarily an *expression* of ethnic unity. However, the proposed research will be able to make this distinction.

2. Considerable literature documents what might seem to be a contrary pattern: church involvement is greater among those whose other organizational secondary commitments are also greater (see Lazerwitz, 1962; Stark and Glock, 1968). The assumption of the theory here is that, whereas the ethnic-related involvement is collective-expressive in nature, organizationally related involvement is individual-expressive. Although the meaning of church involvement for this second type of person also must be measured and cannot be assumed, that it is more expressive of one's individual than of one's collective identity is at least a reasonable presumption. Again, the proposed research is designed to make this distinction.

3. Lenski's study of Protestant-Catholic differences revealed a pattern that takes on added significance when viewed in the context of the theory offered here. Involvement in the white Protestant churches, he says, "is negatively correlated with involvement in the kin group, but positively correlated with involvement in voluntary associations." Among Catholics,

however, church involvement is positively correlated with both kin involvement and voluntary association membership (1961, pp. 244-245, 248, 250). Because Lenski's analysis presumed a causal direction opposite to the one proposed here (though he muses on exactly this point (p. 245), he ended up suggesting that Protestants' involvement *weakens* family ties, a claim that, on the face of it, seems dubious. However, if kinship involvement is not the dependent variable but the causative factor here, then the Lenski findings fit the theory quite well.

4. A range of findings based on region lend credence to the theory presented here. For example, church involvement rates are higher in states where ethnicity thrives, at least as measured by the presence of foreign language newspapers (Wynar and Wynar, 1976) or the headquarters of minority organizations (Cole, 1982). As another example, Stark and Bainbridge (1985, pp. 439 ff.) showed that cult activity is lowest in areas with highest church membership rates. If involvement in a cult is viewed as an extreme form of the individual-expressive orientation toward religion—that is, an expression of the *absence* of primary group ties—then this negative correlation might be anticipated by the theory here. In fact, as Stark and Bainbridge argued, even though converts to cults often join because of friendship ties with persons already members, they also suggest that the cult predisposed are those who may feel most the "process of secularization" (p. 424), i.e., the erosion of primary group ties.

Perhaps the same kind of argument accounts for some of the religious involvement in regions where church-going, instead of an institutionalized, automatic Sunday morning practice, is very much a voluntary act. If, in such areas—the far West is, perhaps, the notable example—the church is less an expression of community than an individual's choice of activity, then the disproportionate number who are evangelical and nondenominational is better understood.[6] Being "Christian" for such people is not the result of inherited community ties but an aggressively achieved, individual status. As Swatos said, "The churches experiencing growth [now] are those giving people a sense of place—individual meaning and purpose in a physical and spiritual community" (1981, p. 226). The erosion of built-in communities, and their replacement by voluntarily created communities, although not obviating the religion-identity link, probably does change its meaning.

5. Related is the upsurge of orthodox religion in America that no theory of secularization anticipated or accounts for now. Even if much of the liberal decline and evangelical increase is little more than the realigning of persons already church goers, we are faced with an anomaly: Why, in the face of modernity and disenchantment with traditional ways (including disenchantment with primary group obligations), are many people turning to creeds that reassert traditional doctrines? One answer is suggested in James Hunter's comment: "modernity creates conditions which complicate the ability of people to sustain a stable and coherent existence in the world. . . . Those particularly affected may then find attractive any meaning system which promises resolution—world views offering reliable moral and social coordinates by which to live" (1987, p. 8). Needless to say, persons yet embedded in overlapping primary groups do not lack for a "stable and coherent existence," however oppressive they may find it, but those cut loose from such anchorage differ in their access to compensatory institutions. As Hunter demonstrated in an earlier analysis of American evangelicalism, distance from modernity is closely linked to being evangelical, but this distance may be not from modernity's corrosive effects—which are, after all, felt by many—but rather from modern alternatives for dealing with the loss of a traditional "stable and coherent existence" (1983, p. 59). With access, then, to neither primary groups nor compensatory alternatives, some persons may refashion traditional orthodoxies. Hunter's review of the concerns found in the literature published by evangelical presses—concern for civic duties, personal health, commercial dealings, and especially such interpersonal relationships as man and wife or parent and child—although not unique to evangelicals, are unusual in expecting the church to be the agency for addressing them.

6. Finally, and as a reminder of just how complicated is the religious scene the theory must address, the area of the nation most noted for church involvement (the Southeast and South Central) is also most evangelical. I suggest, however, that the evangelical perspective of the South is better understood not so

much as an individual-expressive phenomenon but as a collective-expressive phenomenon. It is as though "Southernness" is an ethnicity, entwined in a number of primary groups, and evangelical religion is its expression. A church booth selling grits and fried okra at a Southern festival, therefore, needs only a sign reading "Sponsored by the Church." It no more needs to specify "Evangelical Protestant" than the souvlaki booth in Santa Barbara needs to specify Greek Orthodox (See, e.g., Egerton, 1974; Hill, 1985; Killian, 1970; Zinn, 1964).

CONCLUSION

The real test of these remarks awaits newly acquired data, of course. My purpose here has been exploratory, not demonstrative, and I am prepared to change the theory to accommodate the findings. We must admit, however, that just as there is no single-cause explanation of the church's continued importance in some people's lives, neither can the social scientific study of religion be content with the answer "It all depends. There are as many explanations as there are individuals." We must, therefore, continue to conjecture, to offer our theories and test them.

CODA

The preceding essay was written in 1987 and delivered that year as the Presidential Address to the Society for the Scientific Study of Religion. Soon thereafter funding was granted by the Lilly Endowment to carry out the research outlined. Telephone interviews with 2,600 randomly sampled adult Americans between the ages of 25 and 60 were conducted in fall 1988. The major report on what was found is contained in *Religion and Personal Autonomy: The Third Disestablishment in America* (Hammond, 1992).

The single best summary statement comparing what was found with what was predicted is this: The fundamental notion that the church is undergoing a change in meaning was upheld, but some measures expected to work did not work, and other measures not anticipated to be important in the analysis proved to be very important indeed. The following are some examples:

1. Although people differed in ethnic identity and in the importance of ethnic ties, these differences were *un*related to religious involvement. Similarly, although people differed in their participation in voluntary associations, this difference was also essentially *un*related to religious involvement. Moreover, the number and variety of voluntary associations reported were much lower than expected.

2. The major independent variable, then—the "grid" formed by Low-High involvement in primary groups (of which ethnicity was expected to be a major one) and Low-High secondary groups—was measured not as anticipated but otherwise. Intimate contact with others in one's neighborhood or local area served as an alternative measure for primary group involvement, and moral orientation (from conventional to "countercultural") in the family-sexual sphere served as an alternative measure for secondary group involvement.

3. Personal autonomy, as these combined alternative measures were called, thus became the major independent variable. Not only were persons high in personal autonomy *less* likely to be involved in a religious organization, but also they were *more* likely, at all levels of involvement, to regard their involvement as a matter of *their* choice, not an obligation arising from other social relationships. They were, for example, less likely to have close friends among fellow parishioners, again at all levels of involvement .

4. The general portrait thus emerged as expected. Further documentation of the portrait's applicability is seen in the comparison of the four states surveyed. North Carolina revealed the lowest rates of personal autonomy and thus the least amount of shift in the church's meaning from primary to secondary (collective-expressive to individual-expressive) identity. In this sense, the hypothesis that "Southernness" is an ethnicity and evangelicalism its expression was upheld. Massachusetts and California revealed the highest rates of personal autonomy, with Ohio in between. Massachusetts and California differ in how they arrived at similar rates, however, a difference owing to denominational distributions. Likewise, the difference between evangelicalism in California and in North Carolina was shown to be related to the difference in religion's cultural role in the two states.

5. On the basis of findings such as these, *Religion and Personal Autonomy* concluded with the speculation that the role assigned to American churches by Alexis de Tocqueville a century and a half ago has now significantly changed. In *Democracy in America* Tocqueville saw few important differences between denominations but observed that affiliation with some denomination was generally expected of persons participating in public life. The effect was to make religion a centripetal force, with collective consequences for the body politic. With the increase of individualism in the ethic surrounding church involvement, however, the capacity of churches to mediate political interests is diminished. From being a bulwark against the "tyranny of the majority," as Tocqueville suggested therefore, religion as practiced in churches is becoming increasingly another "individuating" or centrifugal force. Protestantism, along with other church bodies, decreases in sovereignty irrespective of how "central" it may be in people's lives.

10

Up and Down with the National Faith

INTRODUCTION

The last forty years have been the most volatile period in two centuries of American religious history. Declaring what such volatility finally means will be a task for future analysts, of course, but already it is clear that religion in post-World War II America has behaved in a most unusual fashion. Consider just the following features:

- Throughout the 1950s and early 1960s, unprecedented growth took place in church membership, attendance, and construction. That growth peaked in 1965, but until then it exceeded population growth itself, and in all three major faiths.
- By the late 1960s, Roman Catholicism had experienced Vatican II, with its attendant issues of birth control, celibacy, and ecclesiastical authority. Meanwhile, Protestants divided over race, war protest, and the churches' role generally in social issues.
- In the 1970s came an explosion of "cults," religious groups drawing not only on Judeo-Christian traditions but also on Eastern

traditions. Their impact was felt by Christians and Jews alike, as was the equally unexpected resurgence of Evangelical Protestantism. At least 20 percent of the nation declared themselves "born again" and helped bring into existence a flourishing "electronic church," as well as a "Moral Majority."

• By 1980 it became clear that the "mainline" denominations, which had experienced such growth in the 1950s, were now being challenged, even surpassed in vigor, by groups that thirty years before either did not exist in America or, if they existed, did not play much of a public role. How is one to understand such volatility?

Suppose we had a valid measure of the American people's religious vitality for each of those years, "vitality" measured in all possible ways. The results might look something like Figure 10.1. Growth is the

FIGURE 10.1
Religious Vitality in America, 1950-1990

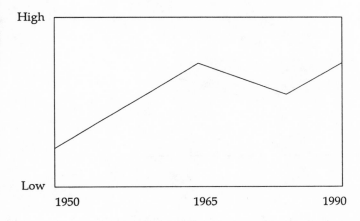

dominant motif in the first half of the period. In 1965 this growth stops, followed by a decline that, sometime around 1976, appears to turn around and resume an upward trend.

This turnaround in the late 1970s must be properly understood, because "Eastern" mysticism, "neo-Evangelical" Protestantism, and all other new (and renewed) religions that emerged in the 1970s obviously hold the key to any religious interpretation of the postwar years. What do *they* mean? Granted, "born again" Christians in the current day may be reluctant to classify themselves with Transcendental Meditators, Moonies, or astrologers. No doubt the reverse is also true. Yet all *do* represent renewed religious vitality. All trace their current energies (if not their origins) to the events of the 1970s. And all employ religious perspectives to some extent at odds with the "mainline" viewpoint that dominated American religion just twenty and thirty years before. For all of their differences, then, these "new" religious movements possess a common element. This common element is what we must understand if we are to grasp the religious meaning of the past several decades.[1]

Consider once again, therefore, the "facts" of Figure 10.1 but shown now in the larger time period of Figure 10.2. In Figure 10.2, 1950-1990, set off by vertical lines, reappears as in Figure 10.1. But now the

FIGURE 10.2
Religious Vitality in America, 1800-2000

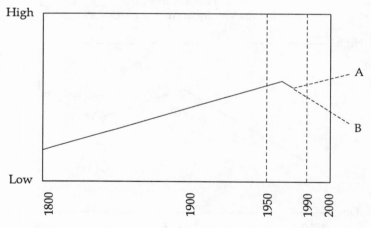

problematic character of the religious vitality in the 1970s is highlighted, not just by 150 more years of history but by the addition of hypothetical dotted lines *A* and *B*, showing alternative paths into the twenty-first century. These lines are only conjecture, of course, but one of them probably will be found to be approximately correct. If it is line *A*, then the current burst of religious interest in America will be viewed as another "awakening." The decade of decline after 1965 will thus be regarded as the "deviant" period, the momentary lapse when Ameri-

cans climbed off their religious incline. That incline, with only temporary setbacks (not depicted in Figure 10.2), is the one existing since the
nation's beginning; the decade 1965-1976 will take its place as simply
one of these temporary setbacks.

If line *B* more nearly describes the religious reality of the next few
decades, however, then 1965 will be looked on as the "great reversal,"
the end of religion's growth in America and the beginning of its decline,
at least its major overhaul. The burst of religious energy in the late
1970s will *not* be viewed as a resumption of religious vitality, therefore. Instead, the fascination with Eastern movements, the resurgence of
evangelicalism, the concern for the occult, and so forth, will be viewed
as the deviant period. Perhaps these movements will be seen as
responses to the realization that a religious decline or transformation
was setting in.

Might one of these two hypothetical futures be regarded as more
likely? The answer is yes. There are sound (if gloomy) theoretical and
historical reasons for expecting *B* rather than *A*. The remaining pages
offer evidence for this estimate. We shall be analyzing the last thirty-five
years of American religion, then, but in the process we shall also be
invoking a religious context reaching all the way back to our nation's
founding. The purpose, needless to say, is neither to rehearse old history
nor to predict an unknowable future but to gain perspective on the current contradictory and confusing scene.

THE CURRENT SCENE

Certainly the current religious scene *is* contradictory and confusing.
On the one hand, nearly all (94-98 percent) Americans identify with
some religion, and a like number assert their belief in God. In these
respects, Americans now are much like previous Americans, at least
since public opinion polling began. This religiousness, moreover, is
observed in the fact that about two in ten regard themselves as "born
again" evangelicals, whereas a similar percentage (estimated) follow
one or another of the "new" religions. (Thus, for example, Transcendental Meditation practitioners, at 4 percent of the population in 1976,
outnumbered Jews in the United States; 1 percent adhere to an "eastern"
religion; astrology is "believed" by perhaps 15 percent of Americans,
other "new age" beliefs and practices followed by at least that number.)

On the other hand, churches have failed to attract significant portions of younger generations, with the result that *overall* church involvement has shown steady (though leveling) decline since 1965. (Mainline Protestant denominations have felt this decline most, Catholicism somewhat less, and some "conservative" or "evangelical" denominations such as Southern Baptist, Mormon, Seventh-Day Adventist, and Assembly of God experience continual growth.) Related signs of decline include the facts that the nearly universal belief in God is now expressed by the public with declining "certainty," whereas more and more of the population agree that, in any event, such belief is not necessary to being "a good American."

In this last statistic we get an important hint to solving our puzzle because, since the nation's beginning, religiousness has been linked to the sense of national citizenship. If this link has been broken—and the argument here will be the link has at least been severely weakened—then the overall decline of religious vitality since 1965 carries not just "church" implications but political implications as well. If so, the religious vitality since the late 1970s may represent not an awakening, not a resumption of religion's incline in America, but a signal of alarm. After all, it consists of an attraction to "foreign" religions on the part of some Americans, a reassertion of particularistic religion on the part of other Americans, and involvement in highly individualistic, "mystical" religion on the part of yet others. If our analysis is correct, then, the new ager, the saffron-robed Krishna convert, and the born-again Moral Majoritarian have more in common than either is likely to admit—or even realize.

EXTRAPOLATING FROM THE PAST: A NATIONAL FAITH

The links between religiousness and citizenship in America go back to colonial times. The First Great Awakening, the movement associated with Jonathan Edwards in the prewar decades of the New England Colonies, helped remove the church as an "official" factor in political life. Colonists of different religious convictions were therefore able to make common cause against England even if, among themselves, they disagreed on particular beliefs regarding the supernatural.

The Second Great Awakening (c. 1800-1830) further linked religion and politics. Democratic in ideology, this evangelical movement served also to weaken the ecclesiastical hold on American culture, but, paradoxically, in further eroding formal church sovereignty, it increased religion's centrality (and thus potential political influence). This peculiarly American trait was identified in 1831 by the Frenchman, Alexis de Tocqueville, and it has struck foreign observers ever since.

According to this trait, an American does not have to be a member of any specific religious group to qualify for full citizenship, but identification with some religion is taken as a sign also of being a good businessperson, a good politician, a good family member, and so forth.

In similar fashion, however, so does being a church member carry the expectation of civic involvement. Out of the Second Great Awakening, therefore, came much of the community organization (e.g., hospitals, colleges, Sunday Schools, mission societies, magazines, newspapers) and much of the impulse toward social reform (e.g., abolition of slavery, women's suffrage, labor reform laws).

Of course, this overlay of religion and civic activity had a Protestant flavor; the majority of Americans, and an even larger percentage of American leaders, were Protestant. But it is crucial to see that the Awakenings, by weakening ecclesiastical control, made such linkage circumstantial. Once sufficient Catholics, or Jews, or Mormons, or Spiritualists got involved in the community, they too commanded "representation." If the Protestant King James version was the Bible read in public schools, for example, that was only because most teachers, being Protestant themselves, knew *it*; the Roman Catholic Douay version would be just as acceptable if the majority preferred. What was perceived (and experienced) by religious minorities as "Protestant" control was therefore not really *that*. Rather, it was influence in secular institutions (perhaps especially public education) of unmistakably religious forces, but forces outside the jurisdiction of the churches.

The result, since early in the nineteenth century, has been a "national faith," an American religious outlook—largely Protestant originally but decreasingly so—combining themes of ultimate truth and justice with themes of citizenship and national destiny. It gave America a redemptive role, a "chosen nation" status, so that as more and more categories of people were extended rights of citizenship, so did this American national faith expand. This history has been uneven and stained with violations, to be sure, as Masons, Catholics, Mormons, Jews, and Native Americans (to name just some of the domestic targets) suffered at the hands of those reluctant to extend the national faith to "outsiders." But the ideological weight was on the side of extension, not contraction. The American tradition called for religious openness, and for the most part it has been open.

This national faith—this "civil-religion" ethic, if you will—makes religious questions political, but it also makes political questions religious. American politicians engage in crusades, office holders are expected to be morally above suspicion, and campaigns for elected office often take on messianic character.

Insofar as the nearly 200 years of American history up until 1965 was a history of expanding citizenship (as immigrants, ex slaves, women, youth, and so on, were incorporated into the body politic), it is not surprising to find a general increase in church involvement during this same period. This is what Figure 10.2 shows. As more and more persons were granted full status as Americans, they expressed their status (among other ways) by affiliation with the church of their choice. Religious vitality and national vitality were but alternative manifestations of much the same thing: a commitment to the national faith. As Will Herberg helped us recognize in his *Protestant, Catholic, Jew,* this commitment reached extraordinary proportions in the decade and a half following World War II, the unprecedented growth period depicted in Figures 10.1 and 10.2.

CHALLENGES TO THE NATIONAL FAITH

Through the years, the national faith has been jolted, of course. Waves of immigration, an expanding frontier, slavery and the Civil War, evolution and "higher criticism" of the Bible, urbanism and industrialization, government involvement in the economy and in international alliances—all these, and more, tested the resiliency of this American ideology. As each test was met, however, not only did the national faith adjust and adapt, but so also could it then reach out to recruit yet more "believers," persons who theretofore had held back in their national loyalty or in their religious commitment. (As one example from the period under review, witness what John F. Kennedy's election to the White House meant: for Catholics, a sense of first-class citizenship; and, for everybody, a crumbling of Catholic-Protestant suspicions. Catholicism became fully "American.")

The smooth line of Figure 10.2, showing a steady incline from 1800 to 1965, no doubt, would therefore be a jagged line of ups and downs if we had the data, but its overall direction would be up nonetheless. The national faith has been basically optimistic, and one of its manifestations has been a steady increase of citizens' involvement in their churches.

THE CURRENT CHALLENGE

Our question can now be repeated. Was the decline in religious vitality beginning in the mid-1960s a temporary setback, and is the increase beginning a decade later therefore a resumption of a long-term trend? Or was the turn-around of 1965 the true signal, with the new religions and resurgent evangelicalism signs of a declining national faith?

One need not search hard for signs that American democratic culture—the national faith—is in jeopardy. Indeed, indicting the nation has become commonplace: the folly of the Vietnam war, the loss of nerve in civil rights, government paralysis in economic policy, inability to control crime, woefully inadequate health insurance, an arms race nobody professes to want, a tenth of the population hopelessly mired in an underclass. Each of these indictments challenges an implicit contract between citizen and nation, and thus weakens citizen commitment to the national faith. Not surprisingly, this reduced commitment shows up also in church statistics.

We have already noted the decline in *church* vitality since 1965, but what is the evidence of *general* decline? Perhaps the single most persuasive indication is the reversal in the optimism-pessimism ratio among Americans. From the 1950s (when it was first measured) through the mid-1960s, the majority of Americans believed the present superior to the past and expected the future to improve on the present. By 1978 this ratio had significantly changed around: the majority now looked back on a past better than the present and expected the future to be worse yet. Daniel Yankelovich, who reports this change in his book, *New Rules*, calls it "a truly historic shift away from optimism to bleakness."

TWO VARIATIONS ON THE MAINSTREAM

It is against this "shift away from optimism" that the religious vitality of the 1970s must be seen. Both resurgent evangelicalism and the new religions are responses to that shift. Together they indicate the probable decline shown as line *B* in Figure 10.2.

The new religions, of course, have appealed almost exclusively to the young. Whether or not the appeal remains, therefore, new religions signal a general citizenship decline because they appear to stem from disaffiliation with the national faith. This is expressed often as a rejection of the "establishment," including of course a rejection of establishment denominations: the mainline churches of Protestantism, Catholicism, and Judaism.

Ironically, however, the other expression of religious activity since the 1970s, resurgent evangelicalism, also attracts persons marked by a kind of disaffiliation. Neo-evangelicals are drawn disproportionately (not, of course, exclusively) from those who participate little in American culture; they are, for example, often persons of low income and education. Whether or not the renewed appeal of evangelicalism remains, then, its impetus, too, appears in part to be rejection of the same "mainline" national faith, including rejection of establishment denominations.[2]

To be sure, new religionists often make clear their disgust with the American political (especially military) establishment, whereas evangelicals (especially the radical Right among them) frequently appear as apologists for that same establishment. But this difference ought not to mask what is common to these two populations, for what they have in common is a basic distrust of the current American situation. The line of incline beginning in 1800 in Figure 10.2, by 1965, had found both groups profoundly disturbed. The national faith failed to attract significant portions of recent generations, some of whom have been drawn into "alien" religions. But it also failed to attract significant portions of other citizens, some of whom wish to return to what they misperceive as "Christian America."

AND WHAT OF THE FUTURE?

The category David Riesman some years ago called "the curdled indignants" has thus in our day come to include many from two different religious groups, new religionists and neo-evangelicals, who have simply given up on the redemptive character of the historic American ideology. Their participation in the "alien" or the "particularistic" thus includes their *non*participation in mainline American religion. It is one thing to meditate or speak in tongues, to chant in strange robes or testify to Jesus' love; it is quite another to reject the Presbyterian, Methodist, Catholic, or Jewish congregation for being too worldly, compromised, or secular. Yet many seem to have done just that.

The year 1965 thus may play a far more strategic role than a casual glance suggests. If it marks the break-up of the historic link of religion and politics in America, then line *B* in Figure 10.2 is probably correct; the future for "mainstream" religion in America is probably grim. But might instead the national faith enjoy a new burst of energy? Is there a chance line *A*, not line *B*, will prevail?

One can be more confident about what will *not* happen than about what *will*. Surely American citizens will not shift significantly into "Eastern" religions; contemplation and inner experience will not replace Americans' traditional concern for this world. Neither will Americans repudiate religious pluralism, scientifically informed interpretations of sacred texts, and a high premium on individual freedoms, which repudiations would be required in any reinstituted "Christian" America. Thus, the color and variety added by the religious events of the 1970s, and these additions have been considerable, may remain as embellishments on the basic American religious model, but they will not replace that model.

The real question, rather, is what will happen to the basic model: what we have called the *national faith*. Will this national faith weaken still more? Or might some prophetic infusion take place, a religious shot-in-the-arm that at once identifies an optimistic image of the nation's future and provides the spirit to move it?

In the eighteenth century, Jonathan Edwards provided such an infusion. Ostensibly reasserting a Protestant orthodoxy, the Rev. Edwards instead helped Americans trust their own religious intuitions. In so doing, they relegated their denominational preferences to secondary status, giving priority to theological concerns leading to national and civil benefits.

Charles Grandison Finney, in the 1820s and 1830s, provided a stirring infusion along similar lines. The problem then, however, was not so much the formation of a counterforce against an external enemy as it was finding a sacred cause common to all in the new nation. Like Edwards, Finney helped Americans find that cause.

Henry Ward Beecher later in the nineteenth century, and Walter Rauschenbusch early in the twentieth, also served prophetic roles.

Beecher showed how committed believers need not deny the lessons of science as contained in the evolutionary record, and Rauschenbusch offered a creative interpretation of "social Darwinism," the so-called social gospel that brought together the do-good American optimism and the mainline religious viewpoint.

Others more recent could readily be mentioned: John Courtney Murray, the Roman Catholic philosopher who enabled persons to be both "Catholic" and "pluralist"; Rabbi Arthur Hertzberg who helped reformulate the Jewish doctrine of a "chosen people" so it evoked more, not less, from the citizenship of American Jews; Reinhold Niebuhr, who helped the heirs of Luther and Calvin engage politically in this world even as they remained theologically pessimistic. All these persons helped shape the national faith.

In recent years, the outstanding figure to draw religion and politics together, to combine spiritual ferment and expanded conception of civil responsibility was Martin Luther King, Jr. The war in Vietnam, persecution by public officials (ironically, sworn to uphold American ideals), and murder in 1968 of course put an end to King's leadership. They also took the steam out of the nobler expression of the civil rights movement, and it is surely no coincidence that these events were occurring as the religious vitality of America peaked and started downward.

No one has yet succeeded Martin Luther King, Jr., in his national cause, and neither has any other prophetic voice been heard on behalf of the American national faith since the mid-1960s. While some held out the hope that Ronald Reagan would get the nation "back on track," it is now clear that the 1980s did not result in an expanded citizenry or an extension of rights to those heretofore left out. If anything, Reaganomics closed doors, not opened them. Certainly Reagan did not inspire the American people by invoking the same spiritual forces invoked by Edwards, Finney, Beecher, Rauschenbusch, or King.

America may well survive as a geopolitical entity; this essay should be read not as an assessment of the likelihood of national existence in the next century. Rather, it is a diagnosis of the spiritual character of that existence. We may still exist as persons, sharing a state; at issue here is whether we will also be a people, sharing a nation. Of course, it is in the nature of prophecy to be unanticipated. Were it producable on demand, we would not need it. When and if such prophecy arrives, however, we can be certain of one thing: It will reflect religion in the late twentieth century—the most volatile in this nation's history.

11

The Fate of Liberal
Protestantism in America

A superficial glance at the current religious scene in America might lead to the impression that, with Evangelical Protestantism on the rise, Liberal Protestantism is being replaced as the mainline religious expression. Not only has the Protestant conservative wing been growing in size, visibility, and attempted political clout, but so has the liberal wing been declining. Even if, as may be happening now, some leveling off of this decline is occurring, Liberal Protestantism's malaise lingers in the form of lost confidence, cautious social witness, and a dispirited ecumenical movement. The bull market they experienced in the 1950s seems, since the 1960s, not only to have disappeared from their churches but seems also to have reappeared among evangelical churches. How are we to understand this shift?

First, let us be clear about the objects of inquiry. As several of the preceding essays have made clear, during the years from approximately 1890 to 1920, the American Protestantism that had enjoyed near-establishment status for a century confronted the forces of modernity and responded in basically two different ways. One of these responses attempted to hold firm—on doctrine especially perhaps, but also on ethic, church polity, worship, and understanding of the religious experience. It was "defensive," to use Peter Berger's term, in its approach to culture (1969, pp. 153 ff.). The other response was prepared to accommodate to culture, especially those sectors of the culture most caught up in social change.

The first response led to Conservative Protestantism that, for all the differences to be found within it because of selective emphasis— some defending biblical inerrancy, others the paramountcy of the Holy Spirit, yet others dispensationalism, and so on—had as a central feature a resolve not to adjust to the changing culture's standards but to hold on to standards it regarded as its own. Evangelicals were, and are, a major component of this conservative response, so much so in fact that the terms *evangelicalism* and *Conservative Protestantism* are often used interchangeably today. The second response led to Liberal Protestantism that, for all its differences, had as a central feature precisely the willingness to adapt its standards of truth, value, and justice to standards drawn from beyond its own traditions.

Conservative Protestantism thus elected for the most part not to engage the culture at large but to ignore it where discrepancy existed, whereas Liberal Protestantism became liberal primarily to remain in relationship with culture. Estimates now suggest that many church members remained conservative in outlook in almost all denominations, but most of the large church bodies at the turn of the century— Methodist, northern Baptist, Presbyterian, Lutheran, Congregational, Episcopal, Disciples—were "captured" by those of the liberal persuasion. Their leaders, colleges, seminaries, publications, and a great many of their clergy toed the liberal line. They accommodated by their concern for social ministry, their willingness to cooperate across denominational lines, and their openness to "higher criticism" of the Bible. Sometimes, then, Liberal Protestantism is known also as Social Gospel, ecumenical, or modernist Protestantism.

The thesis I put forth here is that Liberal Protestantism, in seeking to stay culturally engaged by responding to the forces of modernity, came to a radically redefined relationship with culture. Moreover, this radical redefinition may have represented—and may yet represent—the only relationship possible for any religion seeking cultural engagement, if it is doing so in a religiously plural situation. If this thesis is true, it means that not only will evangelicalism be unable to recapture the cultural role once played by Protestantism turned liberal, but so also will Liberal Protestantism be unable to recapture its own former role. Put another way, the hegemony gained by liberal religion over conservative religion after the turn of the century was a hegemony won at the cost of greatly altering religion's place in society. The fate of liberal Protestantism in America, therefore, is in significant measure the fate of religion generally in modern society.

Part of this story is well known. Argued most forcefully by Peter Berger (1969), pluralization of religion leads to the privatization of all religions, which means that, however important religion might be in the private lives of individuals, the mutual interchange of persons drawn from different religions tends to downplay, if not exclude, their religions. In the Preface to this book, this latter phenomenon was called *moral neutralization;* and it, together with privatization, constituted religion's loss of sovereignty. To understand how loss of sovereignty happens, however, we need to distinguish religion at the motivational level from religion at the adjudicatory level; and this part of the story is not so well known, especially, perhaps, by church people.

Modernity and religious pluralism may tend, empirically, to diminish the role played by religion in the mental processes of individuals, especially to the degree they encounter and acknowledge religious claims conflicting with their own. This we called *loss of centrality.* But loss of centrality is not inevitable in the face of religious pluralism. People may still be powerfully motivated by their spiritual outlook; and indeed it would be surprising if, in a society as devout as America, we did not frequently run into such people. In addition, numerous insulating techniques, from isolated communities to separate schools, help protect religion at the motivational level.

At the adjudicatory level, however, a quite different picture emerges as the implications of religious pluralism become clearer. Person A asserts her religious interest in action X, whereas person B asserts her religious interest in action non-X. (For example, A claims her religious convictions not only permit but may even dictate abortion under some circumstances, whereas B claims her religious convictions prohibit abortion not only for herself but for all persons.) More commonly perhaps, A makes a claim based on religious convictions, but B, who does not hold such religious convictions, rejects the claims. (For example, Hindu parents insist on vegetarian meals for their children in the public school cafeteria, whereas other parents, having no religious scruples about meat, disapprove of such a proposal.) The question is, How do these persons adjudicate their differences, assuming their mutual desire to remain in the same society?

In a certain sense, one side inevitably "wins" and the other "loses." Abortions will or will not be allowed; vegetarian meals will or will not be served. If religious pluralism is to be maintained, however, the winning side will not, in winning, have its religious convictions vindicated and its opponents' convictions discredited. Rather, religious convictions on both sides will, at this adjudicatory level, be excluded—however important they may be at the motivational level. Not to exclude religion convictions at the adjudicatory level is to establish one religion over another, something explicitly prohibited in the U.S. Constitution and implicitly illegal in all modern nations that are also religiously plural.

On what basis, then, are such cases adjudicated? The answer is by "principles" (variously labeled *legal, ethical,* or *moral*). In a functioning system, such principles must meet two distinguishing qualifications: (1) The principles must be abstract, that is, applicable not just to the case at hand but to other cases as well. People need to be able to discern from principles invoked in one case how similar cases, including those where entirely different religious convictions may be involved, would be decided. (2) The second qualification is that, since such principles cannot be articulated in the religious language peculiar to either contending party, they can be articulated only in language *common* to the contending parties, which is language oftentimes devoid of religious references altogether and therefore oftentimes called *secular humanism,* as we saw in Chapter Six.

Now this set of circumstances happens to be relatively easy to perceive in the legal setting, but it is no less operative in any social setting where persons of diverse religious backgrounds interact. Religion may yet be important at the motivational private level, but it inevitably recedes in importance at the adjudicatory level.

Social circumstances, chiefly immigration, forced "established" Protestantism after the Civil War in America to recognize the fact of religious pluralism. Even if all Protestants remained as convinced as ever of their singular hold on religious truth, they were destined, because of pluralism, to see a decline in the use of Protestant language in the adjudication process. At the same time, however, religious pluralism, as well as other features of modernity, primarily education and urban social ills, were eroding the religious motivation of many. People were *not* as convinced as ever of their singular hold on religious truth, with the consequence that the decline in the use of Protestant language in the adjudication process was regretted less than it might have been.

But we are now describing chiefly the Liberal Protestant response, not the evangelical. To a significant degree, Conservative Protestants "withdrew" from cultural engagement, which withdrawal minimized their need to recognize their altered relationship to it. Liberal Protestants, meanwhile, were eager to embrace the culture that was inexorably excluding their language at the adjudicatory level and eroding their commitment to that language at the motivational level.

That account brings us to the present—and to the contrasting situations of Liberal and Conservative Protestantism. One is dispirited, the other optimistic; but neither is quite aware of what its future can be. In the case of evangelicalism, the ordeal of modernity, especially the full import of pluralism, has yet to be squarely faced. When it is, there is every reason to assume that a domestication process will occur not unlike the process that gave rise to Liberal Protestantism. Indeed, ample evidence suggests such process is already underway, especially among the politicized evangelicals who are sincerely trying to influence American culture; their only choice, so to speak, is to compromise at the adjudicatory level with those who share their political aims but not their religious motives (e.g., Hunter, 1987).

But if Evangelical Protestants are slow in realizing that their religious motives are not also coins of the realm at the adjudicatory level, Liberal Protestants have yet to realize the full meaning for them of the pluralistic game they have for decades been playing. Unlike their conservative brethren—whose loss to liberals early in this century left them both culturally powerless and, until recently, culturally disengaged and thus unconcerned about being culturally powerless—Liberal Protestants have remained culturally engaged but not fully aware of their cultural powerlessness. The reason, put simply, is that the culture toward which they are powerless has only slowly lost its Protestant appearance. That slowness camouflaged, especially perhaps for Liberal Protestants themselves, the altered relationship they have had with culture since the turn of the century. For example, there was no compelling reason why, especially since the massive immigration of Catholics and Jews, the Protestant Bible continued to be the Bible used in courts, in public schools, and in public ceremonies generally. And yet the force of inertia kept it there. Nor was there logical (as distinct from empirical) reason why Protestants continued to dominate politics, from the White House to local school boards, way beyond their numerical representation in the United States. American culture, to put it another way, remained "Protestant" far longer than the American population.

Several of the preceding essays discuss why events in the decade of the 1960s led to the unmasking of this seeming Protestant hegemony. But one factual portrait is enough to show the consequence for Liberal Protestantism—and not just Liberal Protestantism but Judaism and Catholicism as well. Table 11.1 shows the proportion of American adults who, in quitting the religious affiliation of their parents, quit religious

TABLE 11.1

The Proportion, by Year of Birth, of Those Who, Having Defected from Parental Religion, Have Departed Religious Affiliation Altogether

	Year of Birth		
Parental Denomination	1931 or Earlier	1932-1946	1947 and Since
Protestant			
Methodist	8 (39)	13 (31)	29 (24)
Lutheran	9 (22)	21 (28)	40 (30)
Presbyterian	7 (41)	15 (54)	28 (46)
Episcopal	21 (34)	38 (42)	48 (40)
White Baptist	9 (33)	13 (31)	29 (24)
Black Baptist	18 (18)	29 (21)	39 (18)
Catholic	23 (13)	47 (17)	55 (22)
Jewish	33 (15)	69 (16)	64 (25)

NOTE: These data are from the 1973-80 General Social Surveys by the National Opinion Research Center of the University of Chicago. I am grateful for the cooperation of Professor Samuel Mueller of the University of Akron for making them available in this form.

affiliation altogether. Displayed by denomination and by age group, the figures tell us that defection occurs in similar fashion in all these denominations and is especially intense among those who were reaching adulthood beginning in the 1960s. For that age group, indeed, the defection rate is about 35 percent.

Now, denominational switching has long been common on the American ecclesiastical scene. Roughly a third of the Protestants in the denominations listed in Table 11.1 have changed from parents' affiliation, and this has been true throughout this century. Until the 1960s, however, the vast majority merely switched into a similar denomination; now more than a third of this third move out altogether. Moreover, this rate approaches, though it does not yet equal, the dropout rates of those Catholics and Jews who defect from their parental religion. (This comparison is tricky; the *defection* rate from parental religion in the case of Catholics and Jews is roughly half that of Protestants, but the *dropout* rate of Catholic and Jewish defectors is greater than that of Protestants.)

The message would seem to be clear: many in this society seem to find it possible to maintain their identities as Americans without church affiliation generally, and without Liberal Protestant affiliation specifically. This, I submit, represents a cultural shift of some magnitude and suggests a future for Liberal Protestantism in America quite different from either its past or its present.

In an effort to learn how Liberal Protestant denominations have understood themselves during the last two decades, a survey was done of the "house organs" of some major liberal denominations: the magazines distributed to members and devoted to issues of how "our" church is responding in one or another area with respect to one or another problem. For the most part, the articles are sensitive analyses; given neither to hysterical criticism nor to naive self-congratulation, they attempt to depict what the church is by describing what the church is doing.

The liberal church's altered relationship to culture at the adjudicatory level seems to be comprehended. The survey paid close attention to three problem areas—foreign missions, ministry to higher education, and pastoral counseling—and in all three, any "unique claim" position seems largely to have disappeared. (See the chapters by Burdick, Naylor, and Mahaffey in Michaelsen and Roof, 1986.) Thus, in foreign missions the emphasis is no longer on bringing Protestant Christianity to those not yet converted but instead is on nurturing "Christianlike" attitudes, behaviors, and institutions in societies where these features are problematic. Liberal denominations thus cooperate with secular agencies to distribute food, teach agriculture, provide medical care, and so forth. In doing so, they relinquish the claim that, by virtue of the fact that their behavior is motivated by their Protestant convictions, it is thus of higher priority than those of other participants.

In higher education the situation is similar, although programs of action, given this new understanding of the church's claims, are more difficult to discern. Still, one after another of campus ministry's valuable past programs have been absorbed by colleges and universities themselves—as counseling, orientation get-togethers, retreats, extracurricular study groups, and avenues for social witness have become part of higher education's own offerings. As a result, liberal churches have ceased asserting their unique capacity to do these things. The fact is secular agencies do them too, and do them as well if not better.

The situation with church-sponsored therapy is also similar, though with reverberations not found in missions or campus ministry. The cure of souls has always been a ministry of the church, whatever the period and whatever its theology. Relevant here is simply the degree to which the therapeutic function is now shared with so many other agencies, and especially the degree to which nonreligious standards now pervade even the therapy offered by the church. It has even happened that lawsuits have been brought against clergy for "incorrect" diagnosis and prescription that, it is claimed, led to further illness, not cure. Liberal denominations have been less involved than conservative denomination (especially "healing" denominations) in such legal entanglements, but this simply reflects the degree to which Liberal Protestant standards of therapy do *not* challenge the wider culture's standards. As with foreign missions and higher education, Liberal Protestant counseling has not only become indistinguishable from secular counseling at the adjudicatory level but also seems to accept this altered state of affairs.

It is at the motivational level where confusion reigns within Liberal Protestantism. Can it be, many are asking, that mainline denominations are no longer mainline? Will Methodists, Lutherans, Presbyterians, and so forth become mere "sectarian" alternatives? Is that their future in America?

Although the evidence just reviewed is hardly sufficient to answer those questions unequivocally in the affirmative, it leans in that direction. In this respect we are in the company of many researchers who have given a gloomy prognosis for Liberal Protestantism. But whereas the pictures of the future painted by these various scholars may resemble one another, the presumed paths for getting there differ and so, therefore, do prescriptions of what liberal churches might do in response. Let us list a few.

First, another set of facts will help illuminate the dilemma. Roof and McKinney (1985) pointed out that Liberal Protestant church members, on the average, are four years older than Americans generally and six years older than Mormons and Roman Catholics. In human, as distinct from demographic, terms, this means much the same as Table 11.1: the young are the primary defectors. It also means that those young who stay do not reproduce at the same rate as Mormon and Roman Catholics. And it means as well that fewer converts are made of the young.

These sets of facts suggest, however, the long-run futility of tightening up on orthodoxy, since it would appear liberal churches lose out not to their conservative counterparts but to the "nonchurch." Put another way, the most liberal within the liberal churches fall away, a process going on in all churches, though at different rates in different layers of "liberalness," of course.

These sets of facts also suggest, as Dean Kelley (1972) persuasively argued, that Liberal Protestantism, in loosening the strictures of doctrine, also loosened the bonds of community. If the former cannot be reinvoked, at least without losing the liberal character, the latter can, perhaps. This is the lesson of the "homogeneous unit" line of reasoning now dominating the church growth literature. It violates the universalizing ideal of liberal ideology, but it squares with the notion of the church as a community. Especially churches that have lost their historic ties to ethnic groups, recruiting a homogeneous membership along neighborhood, class, occupation, or other lines may be a necessary strategy.

Another strategy to be employed by Liberal Protestantism amounts to a backing off from its social witness. Lest there be misunderstanding, let two qualifications immediately be added: First, such a prescription amounts to mere recognition of what is already the case anyway; Protestant churches once may have "delivered the votes," but clearly they do not now. Quite the contrary, those parishioners most inclined to vote in accord with their liberal leaders are the parishioners most inclined to cease being parishioners.

Second, and far less discouraging, the strategy of backing off from social witness makes sense in part because of the very successes at social witness in the past, when the church's relationship with culture was not what it is today. We saw earlier, in the areas of foreign missions and higher education, much of what liberal churches pioneered has become standard procedure, carried on by secular agencies. Hospitals, orphanages, adoption bureaus, employment services, housing agencies, and meal deliveries are other instances. If these were glorious chapters in the social ministry of churches past, their continuation by nonchurches does not signal failure on the part of the social ministry of churches present. What *is* signaled is the alteration in the relationship between church and culture.

These strategies operate on the principle that, in the long-run, churches will depend on community. And community in this day and age in America depends less upon theological beliefs than the reverse.

Community, then, is the keystone. Without it no kind of beliefs are likely to be plausible, but with it many kinds may be. Durkheim was right on this particular point: that religion grows out of experiences with the sacred, which in turn grow out of our intimate relationships with others. As long as societies maintained certain levels of continuity—as long, that is, as one generation's intimate relationships resembled another generation's—then their experiences of the sacred also resembled each other's and so, therefore, would their religions resemble each other and thus be "inheritable."

The social conditions of modern life brought about discontinuity, however, not only between generations but also between sectors of the population divided along all kinds of other lines. Moreover, *awareness* of this discontinuity became a mark of modernity, so that different experiences of the sacred not only existed but were known to exist. Churches, as embodiments of the religions expressing the sacred, found it increasingly difficult to keep up, as much that had been sacred in the churches now seemed less so and much that was being recognized as sacred seemed to fall outside of the churches.

Liberal Protestant churches have, by becoming liberal, acknowledged this dilemma, even if the full implications are not fully understood. What does seem certain, however, is that the circumstances leading to these implications will not disappear: The sacred will never again be experienced in much the same way by many, so these experiences will hereafter be only partially expressed through the religion of churches, and those churches will themselves become more "sectarian." Of course, Conservative Protestantism in America will ultimately be even less successful than Liberal Protestantism in expressing this range of the sacred because of the limits of its doctrinal agenda. But how successful Liberal Protestantism will be depends not just on its doctrinal openness but also on a correct understanding of its relationship to culture, past and present. Protestantism's centrality thus may increase, but only by realizing the meaning of its lost sovereignty.

Notes

PREFACE

The ideas developed in this essay emerged in conversations with Robert Wuthnow when we were colleagues at the University of Arizona. We presented a jointly authored paper to the Pacific Sociological Association in 1976, of which this is an expanded version. Wuthnow deserves credit where the ideas are good, therefore, but he should not be held responsible where they are not. Sociologists of religion will recognize this essay as an effort to elaborate Peter Berger's argument regarding pluralism in his *The Sacred Canopy* (Garden City, NY: Doubleday Anchor, 1967). Berger is one of the few theorists who has taken *religious* pluralism to be a special problem; and I acknowledge my debt to him.

1. Max Weber, *The Sociology of Religion*, trans. Ephraim Fischoff (Boston: Beacon Press, 1963). Weber identified subcategories, too, but they bear less on the thesis here, and I omit them as unnecessarily complicating.

2. Sidney E. Mead, *The Lively Experiment* (New York: Harper, 1963), p. 3.

3. Michael Novak, *Choosing Our King* (New York: Macmillan, 1974), p. 107.

4. Quoted in C. K. Shipton, "The Locus of Authority in Colonial Massachusetts," in G. A. Billias, ed., *Law and Authority in Colonial America* (Barre, MA: Barre Publishers, 1965), p. 143.

5. Henry F. May, *Protestant Churches and Industrial America* (New York: Harper, 1949), p. ix.

6. One invites criticism by periodizing, as intellectual historians can trace infinitely any cultural item if given enough time and a patient audience. I confess to a dislike of such reluctance to cut and tie knots, but I also confess to not being a historian. I am simply trying to discern a storyline to tell a coherent story.

7. Bruno Lasker, *Religious Liberty and Mutual Understanding* (New York: The National Conference of Jews and Christians, 1932), p. 32. A point to be made later also gets illustrated at about this time (1920s). Church bodies were officially going on record opposing the KKK, which was, ostensibly, Christian: "the friend of churches and pastors." The criticisms directed against the KKK could not be merely that it was un-Christian, therefore, but also un-American, undemocratic, and uncivil. See Robert Moats Miller, *American Protestantism and Social Issues, 1919-1939* (Chapel Hill: University of North Carolina Press, 1958), pp. 137-146.

8. Quoted in William R. Hutchison, *The Modernist Impulse in American Protestantism* (Cambridge, MA: Harvard University Press, 1976), p. 204.

9. In Perry Miller et al., *Religion and Freedom of Thought* (Garden City, NY: Doubleday, 1954), p. 55.

10. This, and the next, quotation are from Franklin H. Littell, ed., *Religious Liberty in the Crossfire of Creeds* (Philadelphia: Ecumenical Press, 1978).

11. The word *relative* must be emphasized, and the exception of Northern Ireland duly noted. My broad-gauged assessment is based nonetheless on the evidence monitored worldwide by *The Journal of Church and State* and reported in each issue. Then, too, *relative* religious harmony need only mean more harmony than exists politically or economically, which makes the assessment practically self-evident. Outside of the modern West, the picture is dismal. Littell says that more than three-fourths of the governments in the United Nations know religious or ideological persecution. Ibid. p. 14.

12. The study is cited in Ronald L. Johnstone, *Religion and Society in Interaction* (Englewood Cliffs, NJ: Prentice-Hall, 1975), p. 308.

13. William Martin, "Television: The Birth of a Media Myth," *The Atlantic Monthly* (June 1981), pp. 7-16.

14. In Robert N. Bellah and Phillip E. Hammond, *Varieties of Civil Religion* (New York: Harper and Row, 1980), p. 167 ff.; and greatly elaborated in Robert N. Bellah et al., *Habits of the Heart* (Berkeley and Los Angeles: University of California Press, 1985).

15. A good source of documentation for this change is Robert Moats Miller, *American Protestantism and Social Issues*.

16. I have elaborated this argument in Bellah and Hammond, *Varieties of Civil Religion*, Chapters 5 and 6. For a contrasting view, see Robert E. Stauffer, "Civil Religion, Technocracy, and the Private Sphere," *Journal for the Scientific Study of Religion* 12 (December 1973): 415-425.

17. See Jackson Carroll et al., *Religion in America: 1950 to the Present* (New York: Harper and Row, 1979), Introduction.

CHAPTER 1

1. In addition to the authors already cited, I found help in Cauthen (1962), Gaustad (1966), Ahlstrom (1972), Hopkins (1940), Schlesinger, Sr. (1930-32), and Marsden (1980). I also concur with Ahlstrom that "No aspect of American church history is more in need of summary and yet so difficult to summarize as the movements of dissent and reaction between the Civil War and World War I" (p. 823). The preceding sketch, therefore, is properly seen not as a substitute for a lengthy analysis, but as a device for compressing many currents and countercurrents for the sake of addressing the next topics.

2. Miller (1958) is especially good on this point. The contrast is striking between the editorial ambivalence of the 1920s and 1930s and the rather straightforward approval of liberal legislation expressed today in the magazines of mainline denominations.

3. One more illustration: In 1955, Niebuhr said to a UNESCO conference: "Fortunately the nations with a technical civilization were able to correct the injustices of their earlier industrialism and to perfect the balance of power in both their political and economic life to such a degree that they attained a measure of health which could serve as an antidote to the Communist poison" (Niebuhr, 1958, p. 18). These are hardly the words of a person critical of capitalism on the grounds it is predatorily un-Christian.

4. Marsden (1980, Chapter 16) looks upon World War I as the decisive event politicizing conservative Protestantism. Although he may exaggerate the role of "higher criticism" and its German origins, he is nevertheless correct, I think, in seeing collapse of American culture—rather than theological error—as the conservatives' new concern.

5. Thus, during spring 1982, the *Los Angeles Times* carried a story about "born-again" surfers at the Santa Monica-Malibu beaches. It seems their distinguishing characteristic is that they do *not* fight over space in an increasingly crowded shoreline.

CHAPTER 2

1. Jerome L. Himmelstein, "The New Right," in *The New Christian Right*, ed. R. C. Liebman and R. Wuthnow (New York: Aldine, 1983), p. 22.

2. Peter Berger, *The Sacred Canopy* (Garden City, NY: Doubleday Anchor, 1969).

3. Two excellent sources on this matter are George M. Marsden, *Fundamentalism and American Culture* (New York: Oxford University Press, 1980) and William R. Hutchison, *The Modernist Impulse in American Protestantism* (New York: Oxford University Press, 1976).

4. Berger, *The Sacred Canopy*, p. 153.

5. Ernest Sandeen, *The Roots of Fundamentalism* (Chicago: University of Chicago Press, 1970), p. 226.

6. See, for example, the exchange regarding the teaching of evolution vs. "scientific" creation in *Christianity Today* (February 3, 1984). The several efforts to use courts in pursuit of their goals have led to utter legal defeat for creationists, although they have had some success terrifying textbook publishers and school districts.

7. The near-classic source remains Dean M. Kelley, *Why Conservative Churches Are Growing* (New York: Harper & Row, 1972).

8. J. K. Hadden and C. K. Swan, *Prime Time Preachers* (Reading, MA: Addison-Wesley, 1981).

9. James D. Hunter, *American Evangelicalism* (New Brunswick, NJ: Rutgers University Press, 1983), p. 103.

10. The banality of the change—and thus its subtlety—is nicely illustrated by the comment of Dean Young, son of the creator of the "Blondie" comic strip and its present author-artist: "Some interviewer asked me if Blondie was in favor of abortion. I couldn't answer because I don't deal in controversy. I deal in fun. It's separate from reality." *Newsweek* (October 1, 1984), p. 77. Much of the countercultural challenge *existed* before the 1960s, but not until then was it openly *advocated*.

11. Consider the shock given Conservative Protestantism by Billy Graham's first visit to Russia, when he allowed that perhaps some religious freedom did exist in that society. To most thoughtful Americans, this "admission" on Graham's part was probably seen as a simple matter of fact, a fact since made evident dramatically and unexpectedly. To his erstwhile friends, however, Graham was now a heretic, having relinquished the "evil empire" view of Russia. This episode is but one in Graham's recent career indicating that he has finally discovered some of the forces of modernity Liberal Protestants have been confronting for decades. Needless to say, events since 1989 have led to further problems of interpretation.

12. Richard Quebedeaux, *By What Authority?* (New York: Harper and Row, 1982), p. 82.

13. Jeremy Rifkin (with Ted Howard), *The Emerging Order* (New York: Ballantine Books, 1979).

14. Hunter, *American Evangelicalism*, pp. 59-60.

15. Fort Worth, Texas, n.d.

16. Two good collections of essays bearing on this issue and containing empirical evidence in support of some of my assertions here are R. C. Liebman and R. Wuthnow, eds., *The New Christian Right* (New York: Aldine, 1983) and D. G. Bromley and A. Shupe, eds., *New Christian Politics* (Macon, GA: Mercer University Press, 1984). One must also acknowledge the small but vocal sector of Protestants who, though theologically conservative, are politically liberal. Such evangelical publications as *Sojourners*, *The Wittenberg Door*, and *The Other Side* reflect this perspective.

CHAPTER 3

This essay was coauthored by R. C. Gordon-McCutchan

1. By *cults* here we mean simply those movements and groups tracing their roots to "alien," not "mainstream," religious traditions of their own society. They are to be distinguished from sects, which begin as schisms within one or another of the mainstream traditions.

2. Robert N. Bellah, "New Religious Consciousness and the Crisis in Modernity" in C. Y. Glock and R. N. Bellah, eds., *The New Religious Consciousness* (Berkeley: University of California Press, 1976), pp. 333-352.

3. Ralph Waldo Emerson, *The Complete Works of Ralph Waldo Emerson*, Concord edition (Boston and New York: Houghton, Mifflin and Company, 1903), vol. 10, p. 374.

4. Ibid., Vol. 1, pp. 347-348.

5. Though coined by Chesterton, the phrase was popularized by Sidney E. Mead, whose essay, "The Nation with the Soul of the Church," *Church History*, 36 (September 1967): 1-22, has had more than casual influence on this essay.

6. Donald G. Mathews, "The Second Great Awakening as an Organizing Process, 1780-1830" in J. M. Mulder and John F. Wilson, eds., *Religion in American History* (Englewood Cliffs, NJ: Prentice-Hall, 1978), pp. 207-208.

7. This latter point is vividly illustrated in the negative by twentieth-century American Catholics who *are* religious rebels and whose quarrel *is* with their religious establishment. No evidence of which we are aware suggest these rebels were disproportionately drawn to cults.

8. Stanley M. Elkins, *Slavery: A Problem in American Institutional and Intellectual Life* (New York: Grosset and Dunlop, 1963), pp. 165-166. See also Linda K. Pritchard "Religious Change in Nineteenth-Century America" in Glock and Bellah, eds., *The New Religious Consciousness*, pp. 297-330.

9. Emerson, vol. 1, p. 230.

10. Ibid., vol. 1, pp. 340-341.

11. John L. Thomas, "Antislavery and Utopia" in Martin Duberman, ed., *The Antislavery Vanguard* (Princeton, NJ: Princeton University Press, 1965), p. 249.

12. Henry David Thoreau, *Antislavery and Reform Papers*, ed. H. S. Salt (Miami: Mnemosyne Publishing Co., 1969), p. 26.

13. Emerson, vol. 3, p. 225.

14. W. Clark Roof, "Alienation and Apostasy," *Society* 15 (May-June 1978), p. 44.

15. Will Herberg, *Protestant, Catholic, Jew* (Garden City, NY: Doubleday Anchor, 1955).

16. John F. Wilson, *Public Religion in American Culture* (Philadelphia: Temple University Press, 1979), pp. 144-145.

CHAPTER 4

1. S. M. Lipset, "Religion in America: What Religious Revival?" *Review of Religious Research* (Summer 1959): 17-24; Garry Wills, "What Religious Revival?" *Psychology Today* (April 1976), pp. 74 ff.

2. This is the position of Tom Wolfe, "The Me Decade and the Third Great Awakening," *New West* (August 30, 1976), pp. 27-48.

3. This position is expressed by Robert Nisbet, *History of the Idea of Progress* (New York: Basic Books, 1980), p. 357.

4. Alexis de Tocqueville, *Democracy in America*, trans. George Lawrence (Garden City, NY: Doubleday Anchor, 1969), pp. 507-509.

5. I have benefitted here from Gianfranco Poggi, *Images of Society* (Palo Alto, CA: Stanford University Press, 1972).

6. A good survey of awakening in America is William G. McLoughlin, *Revivals, Awakenings, and Reform* (Chicago: University of Chicago Press, 1978).

7. Donald G. Mathews, "The Second Great Awakening as an Organizing Process, 1780-1830," *American Quarterly* 21 (1969): 23-24, is a good summary of evidence on this point.

8. This estimate can be found in a number of places, but especially in recent Gallup polls.

9. These data are reported in *Christianity Today*, beginning in December 1979 and continuing since.

10. These data are reported in "Emerging Trends," a monthly newsletter of the Princeton Religious Research Center, an affiliate of the Gallup Organization. Cited here are findings reported during 1980-1981.

11. This result is reported in a secondary analysis of Gallup's *Christianity Today* survey data, James D. Hunter, *American Evangelicalism* (New Brunswick, NJ: Rutgers University Press, 1983).

12. Connecticut Mutual Life Insurance Co., *Report on American Values in the '80s*, 1981. For the Gallup finding see "Emerging Trends" (October 1980).

13. James D. Hunter, "The New Class and the Young Evangelicals," *Review of Religious Research* 22 (December 1980), pp. 155-169.

14. "Emerging Trends" (September 1980).

15. S. M. Lipset and Earl Raab, "The Election and the Evangelicals," *Commentary* 71 (March 1981), pp. 25-32.

16. "Emerging Trends" (January 1981).

17. "Emerging Trends" (February 1981). See also Jeffrey K. Hadden and Charles E. Swann, *Prime Time Preachers* (Boston: Addison-Wesley, 1981). The scandals surrounding Jim and Tammy Bakker, then Jimmy Swaggart, coupled

with the public relations miscalculation by Oral Roberts and the speed with which the Pat Robertson Presidential campaign deflated, has apparently hastened the retrenchment.

18. Hunter, *American Evangelicalism*, Chapter 6.

19. "Emerging Trends" (February 1981).

CHAPTER 7

1. Strout reminds us that the Northwest Ordinance (1787) reflected the desire to both "remove religious barriers to civil rights" and provide land grants to support "religion and schools" inasmuch as both were "necessary to good government and the happiness of mankind" (1974, p. 78).

2. See Abraham (1980) for a good discussion of this litigation.

3. Justice White in dissent, joined by Justices Burger and Stewart, apparently continued in the earlier assumption that everyone agrees on what religion is. Some things "cannot be forbidden to religious practitioners," he wrote, "which may be forbidden to others."

CHAPTER 8

1. Sanford Levinson, *Constitutional Faith*, Princeton, NJ: Princeton University Press, 1988.

2. Prudence dictates an explanatory note here. It is obviously not my role as a social scientist to authenticate religions. Rather, what I am asserting is that, if an ideology functions as a religion, it must exist in reality in the minds of its followers. *They* must regard it as not subject to *their* choice. I think this perspective is faithful not just to the world's religious adherents but also to Levinson's originating question: Can faith in the Constitution rightfully be regarded as "faith" if persons think they are *choosing* to be faithful?

3. Robert Bellah's 1968 seminal essay generated a number of survey studies that purported to measure Americans' degree of civil religiousness and, often finding no discernable amount, declared an American civil religion not to exist. It is worth noting that not only did Bellah routinely deny that such studies bore on his thesis but also that his 1985 book, *Habits of the Heart*, treating themes of citizenship, republican virtue, and community vs. individualism, at no point uses the term *civil religion*.

4. I recognize that the word *laity* does not fit the case of either the law student or seminarian, who often is being groomed to join the ranks of the philosopher-kings. Levinson nonetheless suggests, and I am inclined to accept as valid, that in law school and seminary alike much that is taught does not, as constitutional law courses and biblical study courses must, challenge the legitimacy of the very enterprises they themselves are engaged in. Hence the myth—*some* myth—is inescapable.

5. The other instance (p. 176) occurs in a discussion of whether a lawyer (or anybody for that matter) has a "true self" to which one can be faithful. That belief, said Levinson, is chimerical.

6. A large part of *Constitutional Faith* is devoted to the question of oaths, their content and meaning. I am not including any discussion here of these matters, though it is only fair to point out how much mileage Levinson got out of detailed analysis of what I take to be the obscure case of *Schneiderman* v. *United States* (1942).

7. There was the notable exception of James Watt, Reagan's first Interior Secretary, who, given his premillennialist, dispensationalist view of the bible, wondered out loud whether protection of the wilderness was all that important in light of the imminence of the Second Coming. It is a measure of *how* private we expect such views to remain that the public was dumbfounded by Watt's remarks.

8. Alexander Bickel, *The Least Dangerous Branch* (Indianapolis: Bobbs-Merrill, 1962).

9. See, for example, Kenneth Dolbeare and Phillip E. Hammond, *The School Prayer Decisions: From Court Policy to Local Practice* (Chicago: University of Chicago Press, 1971) for an analysis of the actual consequences of *Engel* v. *Vitale* (1962) and *Schempp* (1963) in a number of closely monitored communities as well as nationally.

CHAPTER 9

1. An analogous situation is found among the Karen people, a population living on the border of Thailand and Burma. According to Keyes (1981, p. 8), the Karen people maintain that they are a single ethnic group even though they are religiously divided into "traditional Karen animists, Protestant and Catholic Christians, Buddhists, and followers of a number of syncretic religions." Assuming ethnic identity supercedes religious identity, we would expect more inter-*religious* marriage among the Karen people than marriage between Karen and non-Karen.

2. A related theoretical perspective is the one often called the *meaning-belonging perspective*, summarized neatly in McGuire (1987, pp. 23-36) and exemplified so cogently in Roof (1978) where "localism" (i.e., ties to community) is seen to be analytically independent of (though perhaps empirically related in an inverse fashion to) general socioeconomic standing.

3. There remain two other hypothetical types, both of considerable interest; but about which little can be said here. The first of these types includes persons who are highly involved in both primary and secondary groups, and pressure on the church to move out of a paternalistic mode might be one expectation from this type—as the experience of the postethnic Roman Catholic Church in America seems to illustrate. Another expectation of the first type is exhibited by black Americans, for whom the church is both the source of comfort and the source of challenge. The second hypothetical type, the social isolate involved in neither primary nor secondary groups, has long been a concern of the modern church, in part because of the church's failure to attract such people. "All our studies indicate that those who belong to our churches are for the most part those who belong to everything. The church is not serving . . . a ministry to social isolation. Those who would profit most from the 'fellowship' of the church . . . are those, then, least likely to be reached by the 'respected' churches" (Pitcher, 1966, p. 247).

4. It is important to note that I am not offering this scheme as a replacement for various other theories of church involvement but rather as the interpretive mechanism by which such other theories might operate. The most obvious example, perhaps, is church-sect theory: involvement because one is born into a "church" or because one voluntarily joins a "sect." In the first instance, the church appears as but one of a person's overlapping primary groups; in the second instance, the sect may well be a compartmentalized association, though of course of possibly great importance to its members. Just as clear, therefore, is the fact that my distinction is between *kinds* of involvement, not *strength* of involvement. Similar cases can be made for theories of church involvement based on deprivation, socialization, accommodation, or cognition (see Bibby and Brinkerhoff, 1974).

5. For a special analysis showing this pattern, I am indebted to the project "Ethnic Pluralism in an Urban Setting: A Study of Toronto," Centre for Urban and Community Studies, University of Toronto. Its director, Professor W. Isajiw, and his colleague, Professor Raymond F. Currie of the University of Manitoba, were kind to grant my request.

6. For example, *Christianity Today* subscribers outnumber *Christian Century* subscribers in the Northeast by a ratio of 3.07:1 but in the Pacific States of 6.43:1 (other ratios: Midwest, 3.79:1; South, 5.71:1; Mountain, 5.63:1).

CHAPTER 10

1. I recognize that the various religious movements to be discussed can, and do, make distinctions important to them but ignored here. So could (and do) Methodists, Episcopalians, Reformed Jews, Lutherans, and Catholics. But just as the latter nonetheless fit meaningfully into a category called "mainline" religion, so do the former possess features in common. To focus on the common features is not to deny differences, then, but merely to hold them in abeyance. If it should turn out that one or more of these differences becomes, in retrospect, the important clue to understanding the current religious scene, then this essay will be properly dismissed for missing the mark.

2. New research findings indicated that in North Carolina, for example, where evangelicalism itself has long been the "establishment" religion, church involvement is positively, not negatively, associated with acceptance of conventional social arrangements. Documenting the other side of this argument—that evangelical involvement in other settings is negatively associated with acceptance of convention—can be done with less confidence. See my *Religion and Personal Autonomy*, (1992), Chapter 7.

CHAPTER 11

This chapter is a considerably revised version of "The Extravasation of the Sacred and the Crisis in Liberal Protestantism," in Robert S. Michaelsen and W. Clark Roof, eds., *Liberal Protestantism* (New York: Pilgrim Press, 1986), pp. 51-64.

References

CHAPTER 1

Ahlstrom, Sydney E. 1972. *A Religious History of the American People*. New Haven, CT: Yale University Press.

Cauthen, Kenneth. 1962. *The Impact of American Religious Liberalism*. New York: Harper & Row.

Day, Richard W. 1938. "American Dream Resurgent." *Radical Religion* 4, no. 1 (Winter): 16-22.

Dayton, Edward R., ed. 1986. *Mission Handbook*, 13th ed. Monrovia, CA: MARC.

Fairbank, John J., ed. 1974. *The Missionary Enterprise in China and America*. Cambridge, MA: Harvard University Press.

Gaustad, Edwin S. 1966. *A Religious History of America*. New York: Harper & Row.

Handy, Robert T. 1971. *A Christian America: Protestant Hopes and Historical Realities*. New York: Oxford University Press.

Hocking, William Ernest, ed. 1932. *Re-thinking Missions*. New York: Harper.

Hogg, W. Richie. 1977. "The Role of American Protestantism in World Mission." In R. Pierce Beaver, ed., *American Missions in Bicentennial Perspective*, pp. 354-502. South Pasadena, CA: William Carey Library.

Hopkins, Charles Howard. 1940. *The Rise of the Social Gospel in American Protestantism: 1865-1915*. New Haven, CT: Yale University Press.

Hudson, Winthrop. 1961. *American Protestantism*. Chicago: University of Chicago Press.

Hunter, James D. 1983. *American Evangelicalism*. New Brunswick, NJ: Rutgers University Press.

Hutchison, William R. 1976. *The Modernist Impulse in American Protestantism*. Cambridge, MA: Harvard University Press.

Johnson, Benton. 1982. "Taking Stock: Reflections on the End of Another Era." *Journal for the Scientific Study of Religion* 21 (September): 189-200.

Littell, Franklin. 1971. *From State Church to Pluralism*, rev. ed. New York: Doubleday.

Marsden, George M. 1980. *Fundamentalism and American Culture*. New York: Oxford University Press.

Marty, Martin E. 1970. *Righteous Empire*. New York: Deal Press.

May, Henry F. 1949. *Protestant Churches and Industrial America*. New York: Harper & Bros.

McLoughlin, William G. 1978. *Revivals, Awakenings, and Reform*. Chicago: University of Chicago Press.

Meyer, Donald B. 1960. *The Protestant Search for Political Realism, 1919-1941*. Berkeley: University of California Press.

Miller, Robert Moats. 1958. *American Protestantism and Social Issues, 1919-1939*. Chapel Hill: University of North Carolina Press.

Miller, S. C. 1974. "Ends and Means: Missionary Justification of Force in Nineteenth Century China." In John K. Fairbank, ed., *The Missionary Enterprise in China and America*, pp. 249-282. Cambridge, MA: Harvard University Press.

Niebuhr, Reinhold. 1938. "Editorial." *Radical Religion*, no. 3 (Summer).

——. 1958. *The World Crisis and American Responsibility*. New York: Association Press.

Quebedeaux, Richard. 1982. *By What Authority.* San Francisco: Harper & Row.

Rauschenbusch, Walter. 1907. *Christianity and the Social Crisis.* Republished New York: Harper & Row, 1964.

Sandeen, Ernest R. 1970. *The Roots of Fundamentalism: British and American Millenarianism, 1800-1930.* Chicago: University of Chicago Press.

Schlesinger, Arthur M., Sr. 1930-32. "A Critical Period in American Religion." *Massachusetts Historical Society Proceedings* 64 (October 1930-June 1932): 523-546. Republished in 1967 by Fortress Press.

Schlesinger, Arthur, Jr. 1974. "The Missionary Enterprise and Theories of Imperialism." In John J. Fairbank, ed., *The Missionary Enterprise in China and America*, pp. 336-373. Cambridge, MA: Harvard University Press.

Stacey, William, and Anson Shupe. 1982. "Correlates of Support for the Electronic Church." *Journal for the Scientific Study of Religion* 21 (December).

Warner, R. Stephen. 1979. "Theoretical Barriers to the Understanding of Evangelical Christianity." *Sociological Analysis* 40 (Spring): 1-9.

CHAPTER 5

Bromley, David G. and Anson Shupe, eds. 1984. *New Christian Politics.* Macon, GA: Mercer University Press.

Bruce, Steve. 1983. *One Nation Under God?* Belfast: The Queen's University.

Hammond, Phillip E., and R. Gordon-McCutchan. 1981. "Cults and the Civil Religion." *Revue d'Etudes Americaines* 12 (October): 173-185. Reprinted in this volume as Chapter Three.

Herberg, Will. 1955. *Protestant, Catholic, Jew.* Garden City, NY: Doubleday and Co.

Hill, Samuel S., and D. F. Owen. 1982. *The New Religious Right in America.* Nashville: Abingdon.

Howe, Irving. 1982. *A Margin of Hope.* San Diego: Harcourt, Brace and Jovanovich.

Jenkins, Daniel. 1975. *The British: Their Identity and Their Religion.* London: SCM Press.

Liebman, R. C., and R. Wuthnow, eds. 1983. *The New Christian Right.* New York: Aldine.

Marsden, George. 1977. "Fundamentalism as an American Phenomenon: A Comparison with English Evangelicalism." *Church History* 46 (June): 215-232.

Martin, David. 1982. "Revived Dogma and New Cult." *Daedalus* (Winter): 53-71.

McCready, William, and Andrew Greeley. 1976. *The Ultimate Values of the American People*. Beverly Hills, CA: Sage Publications.

Parkin, Frank. 1967. "Working-Class Conservatives: A Theory of Political Deviance." *British Journal of Sociology* 18: 278-290.

Pierard, Richard V. 1970. *The Unequal Yoke*. Philadelphia: Lippincott.

Runciman, W. G. 1966. *Relative Deprivation and Social Justice*. London: Routledge and Kegan Paul.

Stockton, Ronald R. 1984. "Public Reactions to Jerry Falwell and His Viewpoints." Paper delivered to the Society for the Scientific Study of Religion.

Streiker, Lowell, and G. S. Strober. 1984. *Religion and the New Majority*. New York: Association Press.

Wilson, Bryan. 1985. "Secularization: The Inherited Model." In P. E. Hammond, ed., *The Sacred in a Secular Age*, pp. 9-20. Berkeley and Los Angeles: University of California Press.

CHAPTER 9

Abramson, Harold. 1973. *Ethnic Diversity in Catholic America*. New York: John Wiley & Sons.

———. 1980. "Religion." In S. Thernstrom et al., eds., *Harvard Encyclopedia of American Ethnic Groups*, pp. 869-875. Boston: Belknap Press.

Bellah, Robert, et al. 1985. *Habits of the Heart*. Berkeley: University of California Press.

Bender, Thomas. 1978. *Community and Social Change in America*. New Brunswick, NJ: Rutger's University Press.

Berger, Peter L., and R. J. Neuhaus. 1977. *To Empower People*. Washington, DC: American Enterprise Institute.

Bibby, R. W., and M. B. Brinkerhoff. 1974. "Sources of Religious Involvement." *Review of Religious Research* 15 (Winter): 71-79.

Cole, Katherine W., ed. 1982. *Minority Organizations: A National Directory.* Garrett Park, MD: Garrett Park Press.

Egerton, John. 1974. *The Americanization of Dixie: The Southernization of America.* New York: Harpers' Magazine Press.

Gans, Herbert. 1956. "American Jewry: Past, Present and Future," in 2 parts. *Commentary* 22 (May and June).

————. 1979. "Symbolic Ethnicity: The Future of Ethnic Groups and Cultures in America." *Ethnic and Racial Studies* 2 (January): 1-20.

Gordon, Milton. 1964. *Assimilation in American Life.* New York: Oxford University Press.

Greeley, Andrew. 1971. *Why Can't They Be Like Us?* New York: E. P. Dutton & Co.

————. 1974. *Ethnicity in the United States.* New York: John Wiley & Sons.

Hammond, Phillip E. 1992. *Religion and Personal Autonomy: The Third Disestablishment in America.* Columbia: University of South Carolina Press.

Hansen, M. L. 1952. "The Problem of the Third Generation Immigrant." *Commentary* 14 (November): 492-500.

Hill, Samuel S. 1985. "Religion and Region in America." *Annals, AAPSS* 480 (July): 132-141.

Hunter, James Davison. 1983. *American Evangelicalism.* New Brunswick, NJ: Rutger's University Press.

————. 1987. *Evangelicalism: The Coming Generation.* Chicago: University of Chicago Press.

Keyes, Charles F. 1981. "The Dialectics of Ethnic Change." In C. F. Keyes, ed., *Ethnic Change.* Seattle: University of Washington.

Killian, L. M. 1970. *White Southerners.* New York: Random House.

Kitano, H. H. L., et al. 1984. "Asian American Interracial Marriage." *Journal of Marriage and Family* 46: 179-190.

Lazerwitz, Bernard. 1962. "Membership in Voluntary Associations and Frequency of Church Attendance." *Journal for the Scientific Study of Religion* 2: 74-84.

Lenski, Gerhard. 1961. *The Religious Factor.* Garden City, NY: Doubleday.

Lieberson, Stanley. 1970. *Language and Ethnic Relations in Canada.* New York: Wiley.

Luckmann, Thomas. 1967. *The Invisible Religion*. New York: Macmillan.

Marty, Martin. 1972. "Ethnicity: The Skeleton of Religion in America." *Church History* 41 (March): 5-21.

McGuire, Meredith B. 1987. *Religion: The Social Context*. Belmont, CA: Wadsworth.

Miller, Randall M., and T. D. Marzik, eds. 1977. *Immigrants and Religion in Urban America*. Philadelphia: Temple University Press.

Mol, Hans, ed. 1978. *Identity and Religion*. Beverly Hills, CA: Sage Publications.

Moskos, Charles C., Jr. 1980. *Greek Americans*. Englewood Cliffs, NJ: Prentice-Hall.

Nisbet, Robert. 1953. *The Quest for Community*. New York: Oxford University Press.

Novak, Michael. 1971. *The Rise of the Unmeltable Ethnics*. New York: Macmillan.

Padgett, Deborah. 1980. "Symbolic Ethnicity and Patterns of Ethnic Identity Assertion in American-Born Serbs." *Ethnic Groups* 3 (December): 55-77.

Pitcher, W. Alvin. 1966. "The Politics of Mass Society: Significance for the Churches." In D. B. Robertson, ed., *Voluntary Associations*, pp. 233-259. Richmond: John Knox Press.

Price, C. A. 1963. *Southern Europeans in Australia*. Melbourne: Oxford University Press.

Reitz, Jeffery G. 1980. *The Survival of Ethnic Groups*. Toronto: McGraw-Hill Ryerson.

Roof, W. Clark. 1978. *Commitment and Community*. New York: Elsevier.

Sandberg, Neil C. 1974. *Ethnic Identity and Assimilation: The Polish American Community* (New York: Praeger Publishers).

Smith, Timothy L. 1978. "Religion and Ethnicity in America." *American Historical Review* 83 (December): 1115-1185.

Stark, Rodney, and W. S. Baingridge. 1985. *The Future of Religion*. Berkeley: University of California Press.

Stark, Rodney, and C. Y. Glock. 1968. *American Piety: The Nature of Religious Commitment*. Berkeley and Los Angeles: University of California Press.

Steinberg, Stephen. 1981. *The Ethnic Myth*. New York: Atheneum.

Stout, Harry H. 1975. "Ethnicity: The Vital Center of Religion in America." *Ethnicity* 2 (June): 204-224.

Swatos, William. 1981. "Beyond Denominationalism." *Journal for the Scientific Study of Religion* 20 (September): 217-227.

Thomas, John L. 1951. "The Factor of Religion in the Selection of Marriage Mates." *American Sociological Review* 16: 487-491.

Wilson, Bryan. 1966. *Religion in Secular Society*. London: Watts.

Wynar, L. R., and A. T. Wynar, eds. 1976. *Encyclopedic Directory of Ethnic Newspapers and Periodicals in the U.S.*, 2d ed. Littleton, CO: Libraries Unlimited.

Zinn, Howard. 1964. *The Southern Mystique*. New York: Knoff.

CHAPTER 10

Carroll, Jackson, D. Johnson, and M. Marty. 1979. *Religion in America: 1950 to the Present*. New York: Harper and Row.

Cuddihy, John Murray. 1978. *No Offense*. New York: Seabury.

Hammond, Phillip E. 1992. *Religion and Personal Autonomy: The Third Disestablishment in America*. Columbia: University of South Carolina Press.

Herberg, Will. 1955. *Protestant, Catholic, Jew*. Garden City, NY: Anchor Books.

Marsden, George. 1980. *Fundamentalism in American Culture*. New York: Oxford University Press.

Roof, W. Clark. 1980. "Alienation and Apostacy." In Thomas Robbins and Dick Antony, eds., *In Gods We Trust*, pp. 87-110. New Brunswick, NJ: Transaction Books.

de Tocqueville, Alexis. 1969. *Democracy in America*, Garden City, NY: Anchor Books.

Yankelovich, Daniel. 1981. *New Rules*. New York: Random House.

CHAPTER 11

Berger, Peter. 1969. *The Sacred Canopy*. Garden City, NY: Doubleday Anchor.

Hunter, James D. 1987. *Evangelicalism: The Coming Generation*. Chicago: University of Chicago Press.

Kelley, Dean. 1972. *Why Conservative Churches Are Growing*. New York: Harper and Row.

Michaelsen, Robert S., and W. Clark Roof, eds. 1986. *Liberal Protestantism*. New York: Pilgrim Press.

Roof, W. C., and W. McKinney. 1985. *American Mainline Religion*. New Brunswick, NJ: Rutgers University Press.

Index

Abington School District v. Schempp, 97

Abortion, 41, 49, 53, 70, 76, 81, 88, 165, 166

Abramson, Harold, 140, 141

Adams, John, 41

Alcott, Bronson, 59

American Bar Association, 118

"American Dream Resurgent" (Day), 33

American Evangelicals (Hunter), 49

American Missions in Bicentennial Perspective (Beaver), 37

Ames, Fisher, 115

Annals of the American Academy of Political and Social Science (journal), 108

Anti-Slavery and Reform Papers (Thoreau), 63

Bainbridge, W. S., 147

Ballou, Adin, 59

Battle for the Mind (LaHaye), 95

Beaver, R. P., *American Missions in Bicentennial Perspective*, 37

Beecher, Henry Ward, 161-62

Bellah, Robert, 1, 4, 22, 55, 145, *Habits of the Heart*, 1 and Phillip Hammond, *Varieties of Civil Religion*, 4

Bender, Thomas, 145

Berger, Peter, 45, 46, 145, 164, 165

Bickel, Alexander, 129, 132

Bill of Rights, U.S. Constitution, 12

Black, Hugo, U.S. Supreme Court Justice, 97, 113, 127

Bork, Robert, 128, 131

Bromley, David G., 88

Bruce, Steve, 84-85, 87,
    One Nation Under God?, 85
Burdick, Michael, 169
Burger, Warren, U.S. Supreme Court
    Chief Justice, 98
Bush, George, 54

Calvin, John, 82, 162
The Campus Clergyman (Hammond), 3
Carter, Jimmy, 54, 77
Carver, George Washington, 60
Chesterson, G. K., 60
The Christian Mother Goose, 40
Christian Roundtable, 71
Christian Voice, 76
Christianity Today (magazine), 75
Church, individual- vs. collective-
    expressive cultural role of, 138-
    150
Church League of America, 51
Civil Religion, 1, 4, 6, 55-66, 119-133,
    158
Civil War, American, 15, 29, 31, 45,
    158, 166
Clark, Thomas C., U.S. Supreme
    Court Justice, 97
Cochran v. Louisiana State Board of
    Education, 98, 102-103
Cole, Katherine W., 147
Commodification of Religion, 20, 21
Congress, U. S., 41, 110, 115, 131
Conservative Party, British, 89-90
Constitution, Georgia State, 104
Constitution, U. S. 96, 101, 104, 105,
    106, 119-132, 166
Constitutional Faith (Levinson), 118,
    119, 120, 124, 126, 133
Council on Foreign Affairs, 39
Cults, 55-66, 152, 153, 155, 156, 160,
    161

Daedalus (journal), 83
Davis, David B., 112

Davis, Andrew Jackson, 58,
    The Harmonial Philosophy, 58
Day, Richard W., 33-34,
    "American Dream Resurgent," 33
Dayton, Edward R., 36
Defection, Denominational, 168-170
Democracy in America (Tocqueville),
    72, 114, 151
Democratic Party, 32, 49, 53, 54, 86,
    88, 90, 103
Dolbeare, Kenneth, 4
Douglas, William O., U.S. Supreme
    Court Justice, 16, 103
Douglass, Frederick, 127
Durkheim, Emile, 62, 121, 143, 144,
    172

Eddy, Sherwood, 35
Edwards, Jonanthan, 156, 161, 162
Edwin Meese, U.S. Attorney General,
    127
Egerton, John, 149
Einstein, Albert, 60
Elkins, Stanley M., 62
Elks, Benevolent and Protective
    Order of, 53
Emerson, Ralph Waldo, 57, 58, 62, 63,
    "Self-Reliance" 58
Engel v. Vitale, 97, 102, 107
Equal Rights Admendment, 40, 53
Ethnicity and Religion, 140-150
Everson v. Board of Education, 98, 113

Fairbank, John, 36
Falwell, Jerry, 21, 49, 79, 81, 89
Federal Council of Churches, 15, 31,
    32
    "Social Creed of the Churches,"
    31
Finney, Charles Gradison, 161, 162
First Admendment, U.S.
    Constitution, 98, 105, 109, 110,
    111, 113, 114, 115, 117

Frankfurter, Felix, U.S. Supreme
Court Justice, 127, 128
Friends of Universal Reform, 57
Fugitive Slave Law, 57, 63
Fundamentalism, 45, 70

Gabler, Mel and Norma, 95, 97
Gallup Polling Organization, 75-77
Gans, Herbert, 141
Gay Caucus, Democratic Party, 88
Gilbert, Judge, Georgia Supreme
Court Justice, 104 -106
Gladden, Washington, 31
Glock, Charles Y., 3, 139, 146
God's Answer to Fat: Lose It, 40
Gordon, Milton, 140
Graham, Billy, Rev., 27, 40, 49, 50, 79
Great Awakening, First, 13, 111, 156
Great Awakening, Second, 13, 43-44,
73, 78, 79, 111, 112, 156-157
Great Society, 21
Greeley, Andrew, 83, 140
Greenpeace, 53

Habits of the Heart, 1
Hammond, Phillip E.,
The Campus Clergyman, 3
*Religion and Personal Autonomy:
The Third Disestablishment in
America*, 7, 149, 151
*The Role of Ideology in Church
Participation*, 3
and Kenneth Dolbeare, *The School
Prayer Decisions: From Court Policy
to Local Practice*, 4
Handy, Robert, 29, 31, 35, 36
Hansen, M. L., 141
The Harmonial Philosophy (Davis), 58
Hatch, Orrin, 52
Health and Human Services, U.S.
Bureau of, 39
Herberg, Will, 64, 91, 158
Protestant, Catholic, Jew, 158

Hertzberg, Arthur, Rabbi, 162
Higher Education, Liberal
Protestantism's Ministry to, 169,
170
Hill, Samuel S., 88, 149
Hines, Judge, Georgia Supreme
Court Justice, 105-106
Hocking, William Ernest,
Re-Thinking Missions, 35
Hogg, Richie, 35, 35, 36,
"The Role of American
Protestantism in World Mission,"
37
Holmes, Oliver W., U.S. Supreme
Court Justice, 128
House of Representatives, U.S., 86, 115
Howe, Irving, 86, 90, 108
Hunter, James, 40, 49, 51, 148, 167
American Evangelicals, 49
Hutchison, William R., 30, 35

Importance of Religion (Sovereignty
and Centrality), 10-24, 28, 42, 44,
69, 80, 82, 83, 128, 133, 137, 139,
141, 151, 157, 165, 172,
Privitization of religion and
sovereignty, 19, 21,
Neutralization of religion and
sovereignty, 19, 21,
Ritualization of religion and
centrality, 20, 21,
Commodification of religion and
centrality, 20, 21
"Is Humanism Molesting Your
Child?" (Pro-Family Forum), 51

Jackson, Andrew, 127
Jackson, Thomas J. "Stonewall,"
Gen., 57
Jefferson, Thomas, 108, 109
Jenkins, Daniel, 90
Johnson, Benton, 33
Jones, Jim, Rev., 59

Kelley, Dean, 171
Kennedy, John F., 158
Killian, L. M., 149
King, Martin Luther, Jr., 162
Kitano, H. H. L., 142
Kleinman, Dena, 95

Labor Party, British, 86, 89
LaFollette, Robert, 32
Lahaye, Tim, 97,
    Battle for the Mind, 95
Lane, Charles, 59
The Late Great Planet Earth (Lindsey),
    39
Law and Religion, 4 -7, 14, 16, 17, 18,
    23, 41, 49, 51, 95-107, 108-117, 118-
    133, 166
Law and Social Inquiry (journal), 118
Lazerwitz, Bernard, 139, 146
Lee, "Mother" Anne, 59
Lenski, Gerhard, 146 -147
Levinson, Sanford, 118-133,
    Constitutional Faith, 118, 119, 120,
    124, 126, 133
Lieberson, Stanley, 140
Liebman, R. C., 88
Lincoln, Abraham, 124, 125, 127
Lindsey, Hal,
    The Late Great Planet Earth, 39
Lippmann, Walter, 133
Lipset, S. M., 69, 77, 111-112
Littell, Franklin, 36, 38
Livermore, Samuel, 115
Luckmann, Thomas, 144
Luther, Martin, 82, 162

Madison, James, 115
Mahaffey, Patrick J., 169
Maharishi Mahesh Yogi, 23
Malbin, Michael J., 109, 115
Marsden, George, 38, 40, 84-85
Marsh v. Chambers, 98
Martin, David, 83-85, 87

Marty, Martin, 29, 140
Marzik, T. D., 140
Mathews, Donald G., 61, 11
May, Henry, 15, 29, 31
McCollum v. Board of Education, 102
McCready, William, 83
McDaniel v. Paty, 99
McKinney, William, 170
Mead, Sydney E., 12
Mergens v. Board of Education, 97, 99-
    100
Meyer, Donald, 31
Michaelsen, Robert S., 169
Millennialism, 31, 35, 38, 46, 50
Miller, S. C., 34
Miller, Randall M., 140
Miller, Robert, 31, 32
Miller, William, 58
Missions, Foreign, and Liberal
    Protestantism, 169, 171
Missions, Protestant Foreign, 34-39,
    44-45
Modernism and Modernists,
    Theological, 45, 46, 53, 70, 148,
    163-167
Mol, Hans, 139
Mondale, Walter, 86
Moon, Sung Myung, Rev., 59
Moral Majority, 21, 40, 43, 52, 71, 76,
    77, 79, 81, 84, 85, 87, 89, 153
Moskos, Charles C., Jr. 140, 142
Mott, John R., 35
Mueller, Samuel, 168
Murray, John Courtney, 162

National Conference of Christians
    and Jews, 16
National Council of Churches, 36, 37,
    41, 75, 96
"National Faith," 152-162
National Rifle Association, 53
Naylor, D. Keith, 169
Neo-orthodoxy, 31-34, 47

Neuhaus, R. J. 145
Neutralization of Religion, 19, 21
New Deal, 21, 32, 33, 47
New Rules (Yankelovitch), 159
New York Times, 95
Niebuhr, Reinhold, 17, 31-33, 162,
    Radical Religion (journal), 33
Nisbet, Robert, 145
Nixon, Richard, 27, 56
Novak, Michael, 13, 141
Noyes, John Humphrey, 59, 112

One Nation Under God? (Bruce), 85
Optimism-Pessimism Ratio, 159
Oregon Employment Division v. Smith,
    101
Owen, D. F., 88

Padgett, Deborah, 140
Parkin, Frank, 89
Pastoral Counseling and Liberal
    Protestantism, 169-70
Patton, George, 30
Peale, Norman Vincent, 40, 50
Personal Autonomy, 150
Personal Identity and Religion, 7, 56,
    60, 137-151
Phillips, Howard, 52
Pierard, Richard V., 88
*Pierce v. Society of the Sisters of the
    Holy Names*, 98, 113
Plato, 124
Pluralism, Religious, 2, 5, 6, 7, 9-24,
    30, 83, 105, 107, 110, 114, 130, 133,
    161, 162, 164, 165, 166, 167
Political Action Committees (PACs),
    85
Polygamy, 14, 99, 113
Prayer in Public Schools, 4, 39, 41, 70,
    75, 76, 88, 97, 102-107
Privitization of Religion, 19, 21
Price, C. A., 140

Pro-Family Forum,
    "Is Humanism Molesting Your
    Child?" 51
Protestant, Catholic, Jew (Herberg), 158
Protestantism, Evangelical
    (Conservative), 4-7, 17, 23, 27, 28,
    36-55, 69-80, 81-90, 95, 96, 147,148,
    149, 150, 153, 155, 156, 159, 160,
    163, 164, 167, 171, 172
Protestantism, Liberal, 4-7, 15, 17, 23,
    28, 33, 35, 41, 42, 45-47, 55, 75, 118,
    148, 163-172
Public Education and Religion, 5, 16,
    29, 51, 70, 76, 95, 97, 98, 99, 102,
    111, 157, 167
"Puritan Principle," 14
Publishers Weekly, 40

Quebedeaux, Richard, 40, 50

Raab, Earl, 77
Radha Soami Satsang of Beas, 56
Radical Religion (journal), 33
Rauschenbusch, Walter, 31, 34, 161, 162
Reader's Guide to Periodical Literature,
    78
Reagan, Ronald, 41, 54, 77, 86, 88, 162
Reitz, Jeffery G., 140, 146
Religion and Personal Autonomy
    (Hammond), 7, 149, 151
Religious Establishment, Supreme
    Court's three tests of, 100-101, 113
"Religious Vitality," 153-162
Republican Party, 32, 53, 54, 90
Re-Thinking Missions (Hocking), 35
Revere, Paul, 124
Reynolds v. United States, 14, 113
Ricoeur, Paul, 124
Riesman, David, 160
Rifkin, Jeremy, 50
Ritualization of Religion, 20, 21
"Role of American Protestantism in
    World Mission" (Hogg), 37

The Role of Ideology in Church Participation (Hammond), 3
Roof, W. Clark, 64, 169, 170
Roosevelt, Franklin Delano, 32, 33
Roosevelt, Theodore, 31
Rousseau, Jean-Jacques, 1
Runciman, W. G., 90

Sandberg, Neil C., 140
Sandeen, Ernest R., 38
The Saturday Evening Post, 97
Scalia, Antonin, U.S. Supreme Court Justice, 101
Schaeffer, Francis A., 96
Schlafly, Phyllis, 52
Schlesinger, Arthur, Jr., 34
The School Prayer Decisions: From Court Policy to Local Practice (Hammond and Dolbeare), 4
Schuller, Robert, 49
Scopes Trial, 38, 45
Secularization, 2, 82, 146, 147, 148
Secular Humanism, 7, 17, 41, 42, 51, 88, 95-97, 101, 106, 107, 166
"Self-Reliance" (Emerson), 58
Senate, U.S., 86
Separation, Church-State, 108-117
Sherbert v. Verner, 99
Shupe, Anson, 40, 88
Smith, Joseph, 59
Smith, Timothy, 140
"Social Creed of the Churches" (Federal Council of Churches), 31
Social Gospel, 15, 29, 31, 162, 164
Society for the Scientific Study of Religion, 149
Stacey, William, 40,
Stark, Rodney, 139, 146, 147
State Department, U. S., 51
Steinberg, Stephen, 141
Stockton, Ronald, 88
Stone v. Graham, 100

Streiker, Lowell, 88
Strober, G. S., 88
Stout, Harry H., 140
Strout, Cushing, 113-114
Student Volunteer Movement, 35, 36
Supreme Court, U.S., 4, 14, 39, 96-107, 108-109, 118, 127, 131, 132
Swaggart, Jimmy, 49
Swatos, William, 138, 147

Ten Commandments, 100, 101
The Christian Anti-Communist Crusade, 51
Thomas, John L., 142
Thomas v. Review Board of Indiana, 99
Thoreau, Henry David, *Anti-Slavery and Reform Papers*, 63
Tocqueville, Alexis de, 6, 53, 71-80, 86, 108, 112, 113, 114, 151, 157, *Democracy in America*, 72, 114, 151
Tri-lateral Commission, 39
Trueblood, D. Elton, 97

United Nations, 51
United States v. Seeger, 16, 115, 116

Varieties of Civil Religion (Bellah and Hammond), 4
Vatican II, 18, 152
Viguerie, Richard, 52
Voluntarism, 111, 112, 139-147, 150

Waite, Morrison Remick, U.S. Supreme Court Chief Justice, 14
Walz v. Tax Commission, 98
Warner, Stephen, 27
Weber, Max, 11, 82,
Characterization of religion as "inner-worldy ascetic," 11, 12, 15, 22, 30, 31, 35, 82,
Characterization of religion as "other-worldly mystical," 11, 12, 22, 23

Webster, Daniel, 41
Welsh v. United States, 116
Weyrich, Paul, 52
Widmar v. Vincent, 99
Wilkerson v. Rome, 104
Williams, Roger, 108
Wills, Garry, 69
Wilson, Bryan, 82, 141
Wilson, John F., 65
Wilson, Woodrow, 32

Wisconsin v. Yoder, 99
World Council of Churches, 18
Wuthnow, Robert, 88
Wynar, L. R. and A. T., 147

Yankelovitch, Daniel,
   New Rules, 159

Zinn, Howard, 149
Zorach v. Clauson, 16, 98, 103